John Goddard's
Waterside Guide

John Goddard's Waterside Guide

An angler's pocket reference to the insects
of rivers and lakes – how to identify them
and choose the matching artificial

Line illustrations by Charles Jardine

UNWIN

HYMAN

LONDON SYDNEY WELLINGTON

First published in Great Britain by the
Trade Division of Unwin Hyman Limited, 1988

Unwin Hyman Limited
15-17 Broadwick Street
London W1V 1FP

Allen & Unwin Australia Pty Ltd
8 Napier Street, North Sydney, NSW 2060, Australia

Allen & Unwin New Zealand Pty Ltd with the
Port Nicholson Press
60 Cambridge Terrace, Wellington, New Zealand

Allen & Unwin New Zealand Pty Ltd with the
Port Nicholson Press, 60 Cambridge Terrace
Wellington, New Zealand

British Library Cataloguing in Publication Data

Goddard, John
  John Goddard's waterside guide : insect
  identification for the angler.
  1. Insects—Great Britain—
  Identification   2. Fly fishing—Great
  Britain
  I. Title
  595.70941   QL482.G7

  ISBN 0-04-440179-5

Designed by Jonathan Newdick

Printed in Portugal by Printer Portuguesa

Dedicated to my very good friend Timothy Benn,
without whose help and encouragement this book
would never have been completed.

Contents

Acknowledgment

The author acknowledges with thanks the help given by Keith Whitehead in providing the following photographs: 22, 24, 28, 44, 81, 91, 95, 112, 118, 119, 123, 125, 164, 165, 166, 167, 168, 174, 175, 182, 193, 194, 196 and 197. All other photographs are by the author.

Introduction

Many years have passed and much water has flowed under bridges since I wrote my first book on fly identification for the trout-fisher. In those days I was convinced that "exact imitation" of the natural fly on the water with a pristine and perfect artificial was the key to success. Today I take a more liberal view. With the experience of years, I long ago realised that "exact imitation" is necessary only under certain circumstances.

But what do we mean by "exact imitation"? It is obviously nonsense to suggest that even the most skilful fly-dresser, with the most sophisticated modern materials, can reproduce an exact likeness of a natural insect. Perhaps we should say "close imitation"

On some rivers, and even more so on most stillwaters, the fly-fisher who is able to identify the insects on which the trout are feeding, and then to select the appropriate close imitation, will have a much higher success rate than the angler who has not bothered to acquire this knowledge. However, it would be foolish to suggest that the fly-fisher who has mastered angling entomology alone will ever become a really accomplished angler. So many other aspects of the art are of equal importance.

The Approach

How often do we see a fellow fly-fisher charging along the bank of a river looking for rising fish, and putting down far more trout than he is ever likely to see, or an angler who approaches a rising trout fully upright along an open section of high bank?

Even on stillwaters a stealthy approach can bring rewards. Yet we so often see a fly-fisher arrive at a secluded section of bank, assemble his tackle, and then wade out as far as he can, scaring every self-respecting trout in the vicinity. Even boat anglers are often unaware of how much they reduce their chances of catching trout by being noisy. Noise travels a long way through water. An anchor thrown overboard, instead of being gently lowered, and constant movement in the boat by anglers wearing hard shoes are just two careless actions guaranteed to drive trout out of the fishing area.

As for those fly-fishers who stand up in a boat to cast – words fail me. With a minimum of practice, any fly-fisher can learn to cast just as far from a boat while sitting down as when he is standing. Few anglers seem to realise that they are visible to the trout from a far greater distance when standing, so the habit is counter-productive as well as dangerous. Additionally, the action of casting while standing often rocks the boat so badly that waves spread in all directions, and they, too, have a scaring effect on the trout, particularly in calm conditions.

Presentation

No matter how good the fly-fisher's approach, his knowledge of the water and angling entomology, or even his casting ability, it will all be of little avail unless he has mastered the art of correct presentation. This means the ability to present a dry fly to a rising trout both delicately and accurately, a nymph at the correct distance and depth, and, most difficult of all, to impart, with hand and line action, the correct and life-like movement to a wet fly being retrieved unseen underwater. Most successful stillwater fly-fishers with whom I have fished seem to have this last ability to an astonishing degree, and to watch their hands during the retrieve is rather like watching a master musician at work.

The ability to see fish in the water, or rises at the surface, is also extremely important. The first is an art that can be learned only through experience and constant practice, as the fly-fisher looking for trout has to know exactly what the signs are. It is largely a question of careful observation and concentration, and then to be able to interpret exactly what the various rise-forms mean is a considerable advantage. The subject is covered comprehensively in *The Trout and the Fly*, written by myself and Brian Clarke and published in 1980 by A. & C. Black.

Which Fly?

"What fly is that?" and "Which artificial shall I use?" are questions that have vexed the fly-fisher since the sport began. Neither poses a problem for the fly-fisher with a comprehensive knowledge of angling entomology, but few of us have the time or the inclination to master this particular aspect of our sport. However, it is a fascinating subject, and it does open up a whole new world as well as providing an additional interest during those periods when the fish are not feeding.

But a deep knowledge of entomology is certainly not necessary to increase the chance of filling a creel. A basic understanding of the subject is all that is needed, and it is my sincere hope that this little volume will provide it. It should certainly enable anyone simply and quickly to identify all the more common insects and other fauna, as well as advising on the appropriate artificial.

Why is a knowledge of entomology an advantage? A fly-fisher with years of experience and the ability regularly to catch more than his share of trout may not agree that it is. To him I would pose but one question: Would he or would he not only catch more trout but larger trout if he were able correctly to identify the insects or fauna upon which the trout were feeding? His answer would depend to a large extent on whether or not extensive hatches were taking place. Most trout are opportunist feeders and when hungry are only too willing to accept any food that is presented. At such times trout often take a general fly pattern with confidence, but once a steady hatch of a particular insect begins, they become preoccupied and the general pattern is likely to be largely ineffective. It may still catch the occasional fish, but a close imitation will most certainly catch more, and possibly larger, more educated trout.

For this reason alone it is to the fly-fisher's advantage to be able to identify an insect species and to select a matching artificial, because reasonable hatches of insects of one type or another are likely on every fishing day. Furthermore, it often happens on those waters that are particularly rich in insect life that several different species hatch at the same time. It is then that trout become selective feeders and a knowledge of entomology really brings rewards.

Selective feeders

Every fly-fisher is only too familiar with that infuriating river trout that rises steadily and sips down every third or fourth fly that passes overhead, yet studiously ignores the beautifully tied Large Dark Olive artificial, or whatever, selected to match the hatching natural. But a closer study of the water surface might have revealed that duns of several other species were also hatching, and that the trout in question was feeding on one of these species to the exclusion of all others. This is what is termed selective feeding, and at times the problem it poses is extremely difficult to solve, particularly when fish are feeding beneath the surface.

No one really knows why some trout become so selective in their feeding, but the most likely explanation is that the fish, like ourselves, have taste buds which govern their choice at certain times. On the other hand, particularly when they are feeding beneath the surface on insects, crustaceans or other fauna, they may well concentrate on the species most readily available in return for the least amount of energy expended. At times, too, there is little doubt that they become preoccupied in feeding on one particular species to the exclusion of any others that may begin to hatch.

On rivers, particularly those with crystal-clear water, such as the chalk-streams, where both trout and insect life can be studied at relatively close quarters, it is often – but not always – fairly easy to establish exactly what the trout are taking. But on rivers subject to heavy rod pressure, trout sometimes become so wary that they stop feeding on freshly-hatched duns floating down on the surface and switch to the emerging dun in or just below the surface film. When this happens, there is so little difference in the rise-form that it is quite impossible to be sure. The only way to tell is to observe closely for several minutes all duns floating down over the lie of the trout and see if any of them are taken.

A similar situation may occur on some evenings even on rivers that may be lightly fished, but for a different reason. On rivers that enjoy good falls of spinners of various species, some trout are likely to be feeding exclusively on members of the *Baetis* family. Most members of this family of upwinged spinners lay their eggs underwater, and then the spent and dying spinners float to the surface and drift downstream just beneath the surface film. Again, without careful observation it is quite impossible to establish from the rise-form alone whether a trout is feeding upon *Baetis* species below the film or other species on the surface.

When trout become selective or preoccupied on lakes or reservoirs, the problem can often be very difficult to solve, because neither the trout nor the fauna upon which they are feeding can be observed. Then, local knowledge of the water and the indigenous insect population can be helpful, as, with a little luck, the killing pattern can often be discovered by a process of elimination. On the other hand, should a trout be caught quickly, then an immediate examination of its stomach contents will often provide the vital clue as to what the fish are taking. In fact, I strongly recommend stillwater fly-fishers to carry out an autopsy on every trout caught, as stillwater trout are far more likely suddenly to switch to another species than are river-trout, especially in late evening from mid-summer onwards.

Heavy surface rises can be expected at this time of year as the sun sets. Usually they are wide-spread hatches of various species of chironomid (buzzers) or sedgefly (caddis). The trout may start by feeding on emerging sedge pupae, and then rapidly switch to chironomid pupae. As the evening progresses, they may then change yet again to the adult sedge or even to the emerging adult buzzer. These rapid changes of diet in a compara-tively short time can be extremely frustrating, and unless the fly-fisher is aware of this and is prepared to change artificials accordingly, he will catch few trout.

At certain times of the season, stillwater trout may become preoccupied with one particular type of food for days on end, I still remember one such occasion most vividly, although it happened many years ago. I was having a week's holiday in August on Chew Reservoir, and I had spent two most frustrating days with hardly a fish caught, despite the fact that trout were rising freely all day long. Initially, I was convinced that they were feeding on chironomid pupae, as they were taking right on the surface with typical head-and-tail rises. By the end of the first day I had tried every size and colour of Midge Pupa in my fly box with only one fish to show for my efforts.

The following morning I all but convinced myself that they must be taking caenis, as quite a few of these were on the wing and I knew from past experience that trout also took these tiny creatures with a head-and-tail rise. But this was not the answer either. By late afternoon I was feeling terribly frustrated and cursed myself for failing to examine the stomach contents of the trout I had caught the previous day. In desperation, I then did what I should have done many hours before: I waded out as far as I could into the lake and spent a long time gazing down into the water in an effort to discover what the devil these cussed trout were taking. Eventually, I became aware of small blobs just below the surface film, but it was not until I got the angle of the light right that I realised what they were: floating snails. Fortunately, I had my fly-tying kit with me, so that evening I quickly tied up some matching artificials and for the next two days I had "a ball". By the third day the snails had dis-appeared, just as if someone had waved a magic wand.

I have since experienced several heavy rises to these molluscs, but it is quite a rare event, as they seldom float to the surface and travel along the underside of the surface film more than about once a year. However, the incident does illustrate the importance of careful observation combined with a little knowledge of entomology.

Identification
Within the pages of this book will be found colour photographs of all the more common flies, insects or other fauna that are of importance to both the river and stillwater fly-fisher, together with simple keys to assist in the quick and correct identification of the upwinged flies. In addition, I have, where possible, listed with each natural insect the appropriate artificials. These include both close imitations and general patterns, but I must point out that many of them are my personal choice. Many thousands of artificial patterns exist, and in many cases probably a dozen or more imitations have been perfected over the years to represent one natural species. It would be quite impractical to list all of them, so I can but apologise if I have omitted any particular favourites.

The artificials

Since the early years of dry-fly fishing, two schools of thought have prevailed about artificial flies. There are those fly-fishers who are convinced that the old-established general patterns are adequate, while others are equally convinced that "exact imitations" are a necessity. That doyen of dry-fly fishermen, the great F. M. Halford, was largely responsible for evolving the theory of imitative fly-dressing, and over the intervening years this school of thought has been in the ascendancy.

Today, most fly-fishers accept that, at times at least, imitative patterns are essential, but, as I remarked earlier, I now prefer to think of "close imitations" rather than "exact imitations" – for two reasons. In the first place, some of the most successful imitative patterns developed this century bear little resemblance to the naturals they were tied to represent; second, although it is virtually impossible to tie an exact imitation, it is possible, with modern fly-dressing materials, to come very close to doing so. Despite this, these almost-perfect replicas are seldom consistently successful. This is probably due to differences between the human eye and that of the trout, and to the medium in which trout live.

A fly seen underwater appears very different from the same fly seen in the air. Apart from that, there are two other pertinent thoughts the fly-dresser should bear in mind when developing new patterns. First, it has been long established that trout can see not only colour, but also variations and shades of colour at the outer limits of the spectrum that are invisible to the human eye. Second, it has also been established in laboratory experiments that trout are able to identify minute differences in pattern and shape, so there is little doubt that they can also pick out certain identifying features on insects or flies even of closely-related species. It seems likely that they use this one feature, together with their perception of colour, to pick out one particular species from others that may not be to their liking at the time. This would account for the success of some patterns that do not closely resemble the naturals they are supposed to represent.

A prime example of the importance of colour alone can be established with that old and well-known pattern, the Orange Quill. It is generally accepted that one of the most difficult of all the upwinged flies to imitate successfully is the Blue-winged Olive. The body of this dun appears yellow-green and has been likened to a ripening greengage, yet long ago a fly-fisher discovered by accident that the Orange Quill was very successful when B-WO duns were hatching, and even today it is still in favour. That success seems strange when the bright-orange body of the artificial is compared with the drab, greenish body of the natural. But the reason has now been established. The true colour of the body is in fact orange, but it is overlaid with a slaty-blue integument and appears to our eyes as yellow-green. The eye of a trout probably relegates the blue and green into an unseen background, so that to it the body appears as a distinct orange. On the other hand, some authorities think that the Orange Quill is taken for the female spinner of the B-WO, but I am extremely doubtful about that.

Colour alone can be of paramount importance in some patterns, although why this should be so is unknown. For example, why is it that so often on big reservoirs a fly, or rather a lure, such as Baby Doll dressed with a bright-green body is such a killer when a thick green algal bloom develops? And why is a fly such as Dr Bell's Amber Nymph, with its orange body, so successful at Blagdon? I could quote countless other examples, so it would seem that we still have a lot to learn about the importance of colour in our artificials.

Apart from colour, we must also take into account the physical features of any naturals we are trying to imitate and then try to establish which of these features is likely to attract the trout's attention. Mostly, we can but make an educated guess, but when we get it right, we can be well rewarded, particularly if the feature is exaggerated in the dressing.

Many excellent and killing patterns have been evolved which take into account both colour and the exaggeration of key features. A case in point concerns one of my own patterns which I developed some years ago: the Poly May Dun, tied to represent our largest upwinged dun, the Mayfly, or Green Drake as it is often called. One of the main features of the natural is the extremely large wings, and this was the feature I chose to over-emphasise, combining this particular physical feature with a selection of colours which proved equally important. I also elected to dispense with the tails, as I doubted whether the trout would even be aware of these.

My pattern was therefore dressed as an emerging fly, with the body material extended slightly over the bend of the hook to look like part of the rejected shuck. I also decided to use the most buoyant materials I could find, as I was thoroughly disenchanted with large Mayfly patterns that quickly became waterlogged. I formed the underbody from calf's tail dyed deep gold and extended this up over the eye of the hook, dividing it to form the large, exaggerated wings. Then I dressed the overbody with a cream-coloured polypropylene, which is very buoyant, and finally formed the legs from a black cock hackle. At least, this was the dressing that evolved. At first I dressed the pattern with a white body, pale-grey wings, and a honey hackle. Even then it was effective, but it took three seasons' experimenting with different colour combinations before I was satisfied. It now bears little resemblance to the natural, but when it is cast on to the water and allowed to float along with the naturals, it's a job to tell the difference. The trout obviously find it equally difficult, as it is now a very

10

killing pattern. In fact, for the last few seasons this and my matching Poly May Spinner to represent the spent fly have been the only two patterns I have fished when the large naturals have been hatching.

The design of artificial flies really is a progressive art-form. Most new patterns are rarely born, but are gradually developed, and one of the joys of fly-tying is that there is always room for improvement, either in the method of dressing a pattern or in the use of new materials. Occasionally, too, an improvement or a new method in dressing is introduced to an existing pattern. Indeed, this happened quite recently with a fly with which I had been involved and which Brian Clarke and I introduced in *The Trout and the Fly* – the USD Duns.

These were hailed as the most perfect imitative patterns yet devised, but despite the fact that they proved extremely killing patterns, they never became established as they were difficult and time-consuming to dress. Then in 1982 a good friend of ours, Neil Patterson, devised a new and simple method of tying them and launched them under the name the Funnel Duns. While these were not in the same league as imitative patterns, they did achieve a similar result inasmuch as they, too, were dressed in such a way as to ensure that they floated on the surface with the hook uppermost to keep the body just clear of the water surface, one of the main objects in our own pattern. In practice, they have proved almost as effective, and as they are easy to dress, they will, I am sure, prove more popular than our own pattern. They also have the advantage that they do not need top-quality hackles. In fact, the poorer the hackle the better, as it is tied in sloping forward just behind the eye and behind a thorax formed from dubbed fur, which means that the hackle-points rest on the surface and support the fly, whereas the points of a hackle tied in normal fashion pierce the surface. My only criticism of the new pattern is that

11

all the hackle fibres (which, after all, are meant to represent legs) face forward. But I think I have improved on Neil's concept as I have discovered that by tying in a few extra turns of hackle, I can now slope some of the fibres backward to represent the rear legs of the natural. This not only gives a better silhouette from underwater, but also provides greater floatability. This, then, must surely be an object lesson in how patterns can be developed and improved.

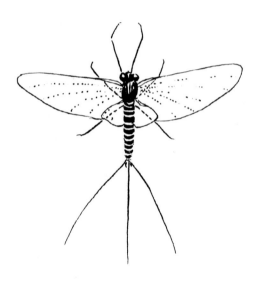

How to use this guide

First obtain a specimen of the natural fly, insect or fauna on which the trout are thought to be feeding.

Turn to page 14 and establish to which group the specimen belongs.

Having established the group, turn to the appropriate chapter and see if the specimen can be matched to any of the photographs in that group.

Unless it is a scarce species, it should be possible to match it to one of the photographs. When this is achieved, check the size and main identification features provided in the text to establish positive identification.

Once positive identification is established, choose an artificial from the list recommended for that fly and refer to the colour pages of artificials to identify it.

If a specimen cannot be obtained, refer to the monthly emergence charts, which should assist a final choice.

NB: The colour photographs of natural and artificial flies in this book are not to scale. Each one has been reproduced as large as possible to aid identification.

Recommended reading

Two of John Goddard's previous books are recommended for more detailed information on natural flies. They are *Trout Fly Recognition* and *Trout Flies of Stillwater*, both published by A. & C. Black.

CHAPTER ONE

The Major Groups
Classification and life-cycles

The entomological Orders *Ephemeroptera*, *Trichoptera*, *Diptera*, and *Plecoptera* include most of the flies and insects which are of importance to the fly-fisher. For simplicity, these can be described as upwinged flies, flies with roof-shaped wings, flat-winged flies and hard-winged flies. Many other Orders also include species that are of interest, and these are listed under *Fauna*.

The first step in the identification of any species is to establish in which of the following groups it should be classified.

Upwinged flies (*Ephemeroptera*) (page 24)
All the flies in this Order have two large, upright, transparent or opaque wings, two or three long tails, a segmented body and a thorax, and almost all have two small hindwings.

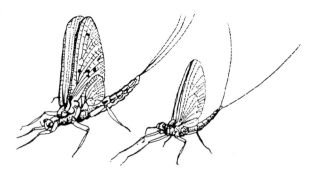

Flies with roof-shaped wings
(*Trichoptera*) (page 26)

These flies (Sedge-flies) have four wings, the forward pair usually being a little longer than those at the rear. When flies of this Order are at rest, their wings lie close along the body in an inverted V-shape. They are similar to many species of moth, but are fairly easy to classify as all Sedge-flies have a coating of fine hairs on their wings, whereas moths' wings are coated with tiny scales. Sedge-flies are without tails.

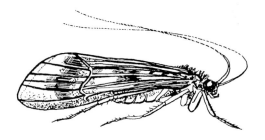

Flat-winged flies (*Diptera*) (page 28)

The flies in this Order have two rather short, transparent wings which mostly lie flat along the top of the body. They have no tails. Two of the most common species in this Order are the common house-fly and the mosquito.

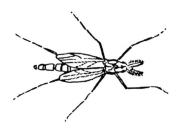

Hard-winged flies (*Plecoptera*) (page 22)

The flies in this Order are less common than flies in the other groups, but they are sometimes important to the fly-fisher in areas where they occur. They have four wings which are hard and shiny and which appear rather narrow when the fly is at rest. They lie flat along and slightly over the body. Some of the larger species have short tails and they are poor fliers.

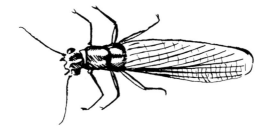

The Fauna (various Orders) (page 23)

In this group are listed all the remaining species which do not come within the four principal Orders, but many are still important to the fly-fisherman, in both running water and stillwater.

The life-cycles

Upwinged flies (*Ephemeroptera*)

Flies in this Order are now commonly referred to by the fly-fisher as upwinged flies. Their life-cycle is egg, nymph, sub-imago (dun), and imago (spinner). Most of their life is spent in the nymphal stage, and in their final stages, as dun and spinner, their life-span can be counted in hours rather than days. Most species in this Order have a yearly cycle, although a few of the largest species have a two-year cycle and some of the smaller species may have more than one cycle in a year.

The egg Eggs are laid by the female spinner on or

sometimes below the surface, where they are either deposited on weeds or sink to the bottom, where they remain until the tiny nymphs hatch. The egg-stage lasts from a matter of days to possibly weeks, according to species and weather conditions.

The nymph This is by far the longest stage in the life-cycle and may last from two months to 12 months or more, according to species, weather and, to some extent, the time of year at which the egg is laid. The nymphs, according to species, take refuge in weed or gravel, under stones or even in silt. Some species make burrows and live in the river-bed. Nymphs moult at regular intervals as they grow.

The sub-imago or dun On reaching maturity, the nymph undergoes its penultimate moult, when it emerges as a winged insect known as the sub-imago or dun. This emergence is fairly rapid. The adult nymph ascends to the surface where the nymphal skin splits along the top of the thorax and the adult winged fly emerges, resting briefly on the surface film or on its own empty shuck while its wings dry. A few species may hatch out via emergent vegetation. The duns are slower to take to the wing on wet and humid days.

The life-span of the female sub-imago in this penultimate stage of development rarely exceeds 36 hours. The dun has rather a drab appearance, its colours being muted and the wings opaque and lined with tiny hairs which are particularly notice-able along the trailing edges.

The imago or spinner The fly that emerges after the final moult is sexually mature and very different from the rather drab dun. The wings are shiny and transparent and devoid of the tiny hairs along the trailing edges. The tails are much longer and the body glistens and pulses with shades of stronger colours. This final metamorphosis takes place on the bankside herbage and, unless prevented by weather conditions, the adult fly takes to the wing usually within 24 hours.

Male spinners can be seen on calm evenings flying in dense swarms. Some species swarm close to the water's-edge, while others swarm further inland or even at a higher altitude. Females ready to mate fly into these swarms and pair with waiting males, copulation taking place on the wing, at least in the early stages.

The males of some species have a longer life expectancy than others and for many days constantly return to the swarms, looking for new mates. The females, on the other hand, die after laying their eggs in or on the water and drift along or around on the surface where they are referred to as spent spinners.

Female spinners oviposit in one of three ways: by releasing eggs on to the water surface; by dipping down on to the surface and releasing eggs in small batches just below the surface film; or by crawling down emergent vegetation or posts to release eggs in chosen locations.

Male spinners also often die and fall on to the water, although most of them die while at rest on the bankside herbage between the periods of swarming.

Flies with roof-shaped wings (*Trichoptera*)

This is a fairly large Order of flies, more than 190 different species having been recorded in the British Isles. They pass through four stages in their development: egg, larva, pupa and adult. Comparatively few species in this Order are recognised by the fly-fisher, since most are either very small, uncommon or only locally distributed. However, the few species that are common are very important as they form one of the major diets for trout in both rivers and stillwaters. The roof-shaped wings are covered in a layer of fine hairs, and the flies have extremely long antennae, sometimes more than three times the length of the body.

The egg Eggs are laid by the adult female in large gelatinous masses which often form rafts on the water surface and drift until they adhere to emergent vegetation. Some species lay their eggs on, or crawl down, emergent vegetation. The eggs hatch into tiny larvae after 10-12 days.

The larva The larvae are fascinating creatures. Those of most species live in cases which they build from any freely-available materials, such as tiny pieces of stick, weed-stems, leaves, tiny stones, gravel or even tiny discarded shells. Species living in running water tend to make their cases from heavy materials that will prevent them being swept along with the current, while those living in stillwater usually make their cases from lighter materials. Some species are free-swimming. They do not build cases, but live in the stones or detritus on the bottom. Some of them build shelters and form a funnel-shaped web to channel food to them. The greater part of their life is spent in this stage.

The pupa This stage may last for several days. The fully-formed pupa has a paddle-shaped pair of front legs fringed with hairs with which it can propel itself. Some species swim up and hatch at the surface in open water, where they are readily available to the trout. Others undertake a longer journey, either to the shore or to emergent vegetation where metamorphosis into the adult takes place. To achieve this, gas, possibly air, is pumped into the pupal case, which then inflates until it splits along the top and the adult winged fly is able to emerge.

The adult Like the upwinged flies, the adult sedge- or caddis-flies vary tremendously in size according to species. They are rather drab-looking, the bodies of most species varying from grey through brown to green. The wings of some are mottled or patterned, while others are quite plain. The colour varies from black to brown through to grey. Many species in this Order are nocturnal, hatching and possibly even egg-laying during darkness. Fortunately for the fisherman, most of the common species hatch and oviposit during daylight. While most of them hatch during early or late evening, some species do emerge in the afternoon. The adults of species that emerge in open water are immediately available to trout, while both these and other species are again available when they return to the water to oviposit. Unlike the upwinged flies, the adults have rudimentary mouths which are able to absorb at least liquid, and some species live for many weeks. Males and possibly females of some species form swarms, where they eventually pair up and mate. Copulation often takes place on the wing, with the female supporting the male, but eventually they sink to the ground where the union is completed.

Flat-winged flies (*Diptera*)

This is an extremely large and complex Order and includes such common species as the House-fly, Bluebottle and Dung-fly, all of which are of terrestrial origin. It also includes a few aquatic species such as the Mosquitoes, Reed Smuts and Midges. The life-cycles of the terrestrial species are of no interest to the fly-fisher, but at least two genera of aquatic members of this group are important.

The Reed Smuts (*Simulium*) These tiny black flies are found only in running water, but although they are an important food source for the trout, as they often hatch out in vast numbers over long periods, they are hardly a favourite of the fly-fisherman. Because of their minute size, they are all but impossible to imitate with fur and feather. Even today they are referred to by many fly-fishers as the "angler's curse", or the "black curse". The eggs, which are laid underwater, hatch within a few days and small worm-like larvae emerge. As these develop, they form funnel-shaped cones in which to live and pupate. These are attached to weed-stems. As a pupa matures, so its case splits and the adult ascends to the surface in a bubble of gas which bursts as it reaches the surface, leaving the fly dry and ready to take to the wing.

The Midges (*Chironomids*) Better known in fly-fishing circles as Buzzers, these small to medium-sized insects are rather gnat-like, except that they have quite large cylindrically-shaped bodies with two transparent wings lying flat along the top. This is a relatively large Family, with more than 380 British species, most of them of aquatic origin. They form a major part of the trout's diet in stillwater, but it has only recently been realised that they are also an important food source for trout in running water. (River fly-fishers take note!) The eggs are deposited on the surface where they form rafts that float while the eggs mature. The eggs hatch in a matter of days and the young larvae descend to the bottom. A few species are free-swimming, but most make tubes of mud or sand or form burrows on the bottom. The larvae of some of the larger species are more than an inch long. Their colour varies from pale-green through brown to a vivid red.

The worm-like larva goes through four moults or instars before it finally pupates within its burrow or case. The pupal stage lasts but a few days. Then, when conditions are right, the pupa swims to the surface, where it rests briefly before the pupal case splits along the thorax and the adult winged fly emerges and flies off.

The pupae are vulnerable to trout as they swim to the surface and even more so as they hang vertically beneath the surface film before emerging. They adopt a horizontal position in the surface before emerging, and it is during this period that they are often responsible for most of the heavy early-morning or late-evening rises on stillwater. These usually occur under calm conditions, as there is then often a heavy surface film which the emerging pupae have difficulty in breaking through, and so are available to the trout for quite a long period. The larger species are generally found in stillwater, where they hatch either in early morning or late evening. Most of the smaller species hatch throughout the day or, in rivers, also in the evening.

Hard-winged flies (*Plecoptera*)

This is a relatively small Order of flies of a little more than 30 species. They are commonly referred to as Stoneflies. They are not so common as most flies in the other groups, but they are certainly important where they do occur in abundance. They vary in size from the Needle Fly, the smallest in the group, which is a little over a ¼ inch long, to the Large Stonefly, which is well over an inch. The adults have four wings which are hard and shiny and conspicuously veined. These are long and slim and lie along the top of and, in some species, slightly around the body. The life-span of these flies varies from one to probably three years.

The egg Eggs are deposited on the surface by the female but quickly sink to the bottom, where they lodge between stones or boulders. They hatch in a matter of days or, in some cases, weeks, according to species.

The nymph The nymphs are tiny when they first hatch, but grow rapidly. They are robust creatures, but rather lethargic. In many areas they are known as creepers. They have two short stubby tails and two quite long antennae on top of their heads. The nymph stage can last for many months or, in the case of some of the larger species, for more than two years.

The wing-cases become more prominent as the nymphs approach maturity. Then the mature nymph crawls either to the shore or to a convenient post, boulder or other obstruction above the surface, where the nymphal case splits along the thorax and the fully winged adult emerges.

The adult The life-span of winged adults varies according to species from many days to several weeks, but they never wander far from water. They are poor fliers and mate at rest. In fact, some of the larger male species have wings so short that they are incapable of flight.

Most species in this Order are an overall brownish colour with yellow or cream markings and heavily-veined wings. However, at least two species are bright yellow. The fish seem to regard the nymphs as great delicacies, feeding on them at every opportunity, particularly during their shoreward migration. The adults are available to the trout only when the females return to the water to lay their eggs. They accomplish this by dipping or by fluttering along the surface and releasing eggs in small batches.

The Fauna

This group embraces all the remaining Orders which include flies, insects and other fauna of interest to the fly-fisherman. Some may have only one genus of value, while others may have many genera. However, many of the fauna in these Orders are of great importance both to trout and fly-fisher. They are all described in detail in the appropriate chapter. The Orders are listed here according to their importance:

Crustacea: Shrimps, Water Louse
Hemiptera: Water Bugs, Corixids
Odonata: Dragonflies, Damselflies
Coleoptera: Beetles
Megaloptera: Alder Flies
Hymenoptera: Wasps, Ants
Orthoptera: Grasshoppers
Arachnidae: Spiders
Lepidoptera: Moths
Neuroptera: Lacewings.

All these Orders, except *Crustacea* and *Arachnidae*, belong to the Class *Insecta*. All Classes are divided into Orders, then into Families and Genera, and finally into Species. Thus:

Mayfly	Hawthorn Fly
Class: *Insecta*	Class: *Insecta*
Order: *Ephemeroptera*	Order: *Diptera*
Family: *Ephemeridae*	Family: *Bibionidae*
Genus: *Ephemera*	Genus: *Bibio*
Species: *Danica*	Species: *Marci*

CHAPTER TWO

The Upwinged Flies

(*Ephemeroptera*)

This Order has relatively few species compared with some of the larger Orders, and the fly-fisher may be misled into assuming that identification is therefore simpler. Unfortunately, this is not so. While it is a small Order, a large percentage of its genera and species are very important indeed. Furthermore, its species, unlike those of other Orders, have two stages to be identified in their adult winged form, the sub-imago (dun) and the imago (spinner). It is also important on occasion to be able to classify males and females separately.

The fly-fisher should have little initial difficulty in designating flies to this Order, as they are the only flies he is likely to see with large upright wings and two or three relatively large tails. Once a specimen has been established as belonging to the *Ephemeroptera*, the next step is to establish to which of six sections it belongs within that Order. Each section is in turn sub-divided into groups, each group embracing certain physical features. By a process of elimination it is possible to establish to which group the specimen belongs. Most groups contain several species, so it is then necessary to narrow the field further, first by size and then by deciding whether the specimen is male, female, dun, or spinner.

The final identification may have to be made by colour alone. This can be difficult or misleading, as colour may vary from specimen to specimen, or according to the time of season, or depending on

air temperature. The colours given in these keys
are "average"

The size of an upwinged fly is often of considerable help in quick identification, so an average-
size silhouette is given for each species. However,
since the males are always a little smaller than the
females, it is wise first to establish the sex. The five
size silhouettes used are as in Drawing 1.

Size 1: Very large.

Size 2: Large.

Size 3: Medium-large.

Size 4: Medium.

Size 5: Small.

Drawing 1 size key for upwinged flies

Before an attempt is made to identify a specimen belonging to this Order, it is good practice first to establish whether it is a dun or a spinner, and then whether it is male or female. The dun has opaque, veined wings lined along their trailing edges with tiny hairs, and the body colour tends to be on the dull side. The spinners have shiny, clear, veined wings, and the body colour is bright and shiny. They also have much longer tails. It is a fairly simple matter to identify the sexes, as the compound eyes, or oculi, of the males are much larger and extend over the top of the head. In addition, the males have a substantial pair of claspers beneath the tail, attached to the penultimate body segment, which, except on some of the tiny species, can be seen clearly with the naked eye.

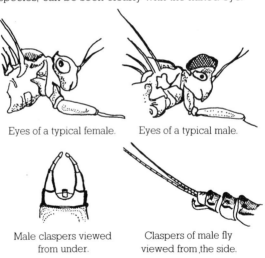

Eyes of a typical female.　　Eyes of a typical male.

Male claspers viewed　　Claspers of male fly
from under.　　viewed from the side.

Drawing 2 sexing the Ephemeroptera

The physical features of all the flies in this Order are:

Head This is often wider than it is long, and much of it is taken up with the eye structure. These flies have no mouths and are incapable of feeding as adults, which probably accounts for the very short life-span of this final stage.

Thorax This is connected to the head by a short neck and consists of three segments. The forward segment carries the forelegs; the middle segment carries the median legs and wings; and the rear segment supports the rear legs.

Abdomen The main body of the fly consists of 10 segments. The ninth segment carries the claspers of the male fly, while the tenth segment of both sexes carries the tails. The upper part of the body is referred to as the dorsum, while the underbody is called the venter.

Wings These rise more or less straight up from the thorax of the fly and are usually about the same length as the body. Some species have upright hindwings about a quarter the length of the main wing, while others have small oval or spur-shaped hindwings and four species have no hindwings at all. The wings are heavily veined and the pattern of the venation can sometimes assist in identification.

Tails Some species have two tails, while others have three. These are often faintly ringed or barred in a dark colour and are fairly long in most species. The tails of the spinners are always much longer than those of the duns. In cold weather the tails of the duns are often quite short immediately after emergence, but they gradually lengthen over the next few hours.

Legs Like all the flies in the Class *Insecta*, they have six legs. The front, or anterior, legs are always considerably longer than the others.

NAME KEY FOR THE UPWINGED FLIES

Present angling name	Former angling name	Entomological name	Popular name for female spinner
Mayfly	Green Drake	*Ephemera danica* *Ephemera vulgata*	Spent Gnat or Grey Drake
Large Dark Olive	Large Spring Olive	*Baetis rhodani*	Large Dark Olive Spinner or Red Spinner
Iron Blue	Iron Blue	*Baetis niger* or **Baetis muticus/pumilus*	Iron Blue Spinner Little Claret Spinner
Medium Olive	Medium Olive or Blue Dun	*Baetis vernus, B. tenax* or *B. buceratus*	Medium Olive Spinner
Small Dark Olive	Summer Olive or July Dun	*Baetis scambus*	Small Red Spinner or Small Dark Olive Spinner
Pale Watery	Pale Watery	**Baetis bioculatus/fuscatus*	Golden Spinner or Pale Watery Spinner
Yellow Evening Dun	Yellow Evening Dun	*Ephemerella notata*	Yellow Evening Spinner
Blue-winged Olive	Blue-winged Olive	*Ephemerella ignita*	Sherry Spinner
Small Spurwing	Little Sky-blue or Pale Watery	*Centropilum luteolum*	Little Amber Spinner

28

Large Spurwing	Blue-winged Pale Watery	*Centroptilum pennulatum*	Large Amber Spinner
Pale Evening Dun	—	*Procloeon bifidum/ pseudorufulum*	Pale Evening Spinner
Pond Olive	Pond Olive	*Cloeon dipterum*	Pond Olive Spinner or Apricot Spinner
Lake Olive	Lake Olive	*Cloeon simile*	Lake Olive Spinner
March Brown	March Brown	*Rithrogena germanica/ haarupi*	March Brown Spinner
Olive Upright	Olive Upright	*Rithrogena semicolorata*	Yellow Upright
Yellow May Dun	Little Yellow May Dun or Yellow Hawk	*Heptagenia sulphurea*	Yellow May Spinner
Dusky Yellowstreak	Dark Dun	*Heptagenia lateralis*	Dusky Yellowstreak Spinner
Turkey Brown	Turkey Brown	*Paraleptophlebia submarginata*	Turkey Brown Spinner
Purple Dun	—	*Paraleptophlebia cincta*	Purple Spinner
Ditch Dun	—	*Habrophlebia fusca*	Ditch Spinner
Claret Dun	Claret Dun	*Leptophlebia vespertina*	Claret Spinner
Sepia Dun	—	*Leptophlebia marginata*	Sepia Spinner

NAME KEY FOR THE UPWINGED FLIES Continued

Present angling name	Former angling name	Entomological name	Popular name for female spinner
Autumn Dun	August Dun	*Ecdyonurus dispar*	Autumn Spinner or Large Red Spinner
Large Brook Dun	—	*Ecdyonurus torrentis*	Large Brook Spinner or Large Red Spinner
Large Summer Dun	Summer Mayfly	*Siphlonurus lacustris* *S. alternatus/linnaeanus S. armatus	Great Red Spinner
Large Green Dun	Large Green Dun	*Ecdyonurus insignis*	Large Green Spinner
Late March Brown	Late or False March Brown	*Ecdyonurus venosus*	Large Red Spinner
Caenis or Broadwing	Angler's Curse or White Midge	*Caenis* and *Brachycercus spp*	Caenis Spinner or Broadwing Spinner

*Species marked with an asterisk have been re-named. The asterisk marks the new scientific nomenclature, followed by the old species name.

This list of upwinged flies includes only the more common species of particular interest to fly-fishermen. It does not include any of the rare or very local species.

Specific imitative patterns are given in the individual keys, but many excellent general patterns are available to represent the duns in this Order. The best of these are: **Kite's Imperial**; **Gold-ribbed Hare's Ear** (winged); **Super Grizzly** (Goddard); **Funnel Dun** (Patterson); and **Beacon Beige** (Dean). A good pattern to represent most of the spinners is a **Pheasant Tail Spinner**.

Details of certain physical features, together with the accompanying illustrations, may help budding angler/entomologists to a more positive identification of some upwinged flies. Many species have large upright hindwings, most of which have a prominent costal projection on the lower leading edge (*Drawing 3*). However, four species are without this feature (*Drawings 4, 5, 6*). They are the **Turkey Brown** (*Paraleptophlebia submarginata*), **Purple Dun** (*Paraleptophlebia cincta*), **Claret Dun** (*Leptophlebia vespertina*), and **Sepia Dun** (*Leptophlebia marginata*)

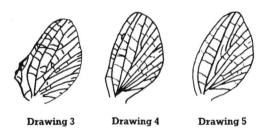

Drawing 3   **Drawing 4**   **Drawing 5**

The large upright hindwings in the first three species of this group are narrower (*Drawings 4 and 5*) than the hindwings of *Leptophlebia marginata* (*Drawing 6*).

One of the species which has large hindwings with costal projections also has an extremely

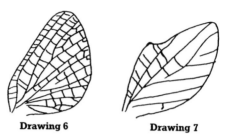

Drawing 6   **Drawing 7**

prominent costal projection higher up on the
leading edge of the hindwing, so it cannot be
confused with any other species, apart, perhaps,
from *E. ignita*, which has a fairly prominent
projection. This is the **Ditch Dun** (*Habrophlebia
fusca*) (*Drawing 7*).

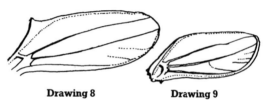

Drawing 8   **Drawing 9**

Most of the medium-to-small upwinged flies
have either small hindwings or none at all. Most of
those that do have hindwings come within the
genus *Baetis*, and these have small, oval-shaped
hindwings with a tiny spur on top of the leading-
edge (*Drawing 8*). However, one species, the fairly
rare *B. atrebatinus*, has no spur at all (*Drawing 9*).
Two other species of upwinged fly that are
extremely similar are from the *Centroptilum*
genus, but a low-powered magnifying glass en-
ables them to be quickly classified, as they have
tiny spur-shaped hindwings (*Drawings 10, 11*).

Drawing 10
Centroptilum luteolum

Drawing 11
Centroptilum pennulatum

The flies in the *Baetis* genus are similar to flies in some other genera, but a useful and infallible method of identifying the *Baetidae* is closely to examine the venation along the trailing edges of the main wings. All species in this genus have tiny double intercalary veins (*Drawing 12*), while those in the *Centroptilum* genus and one or two others have single intercalary veins (*Drawing 13*). Note the relatively tiny hindwings in these two genera.

Drawing 12   **Drawing 13**

Two of the most common species of upwinged fly found on stillwater are the **Lake Olive** (*Cloeon simile*) and the **Pond Olive** (*Cloeon dipterum*). A close look, preferably with a glass, at the top leading edge of the main wings of the Pond Olive will show that it has only three to five small cross-veins (*Drawing 15*), whereas the Lake Olive has nine to eleven (*Drawing 14*). The wings of the female spinner also have a broad band of yellow-olive along the leading edges.

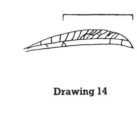

Drawing 14

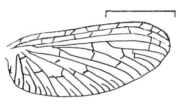

Drawing 15

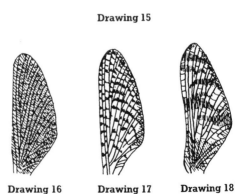

Drawing 16   **Drawing 17**   **Drawing 18**

At least three species of the *Ecdyonurus* genera are difficult to tell apart, but the colours and bandings of the wings can be of great assistance. The wings of *Ecdyonurus dispar* are uniformly brownish-yellow and the cross-veins are only finely bordered with black (*Drawing 16*). On the wings of *Ecdyonurus venosus*, the cross-veins are strongly bordered with black, giving a banded or mottled appearance (*Drawing 17*). While the wings of *Ecdyonurus torrentis* also appear mottled, they also have several definite blackish transverse bands (*Drawing 18*)

Keys to the Upwinged Flies and how to use them

Once the specimen to be identified has been confirmed to be an upwinged fly, refer to page 25 (*Drawing 1*) and establish its size. The first half of the keys covers duns and spinners of medium-large size up to very large. The second half includes all the smaller duns and spinners, from medium size down to very small. However, there are a few exceptions. The Large Dark Olive and the Large Spurwing are both of medium-large size, but they come within the second half because they both have very small oval or spur-shaped hind-wings. If a specimen cannot be identified as coming within either the first half or the second half, it may come within Section 6, which includes some of the more local or uncommon species, which vary in size.

Having established which half the specimen is from, consult the list below and, according to the number of tails and the size and shape of the hindwings, and in some cases the colour of the wings, narrow its identity down to a group. Once it has been classified within a group, turn to the pages indicated for the final identification.

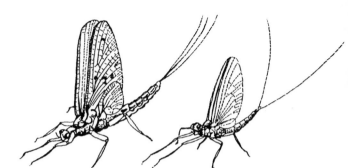

Drawing 19:
Imago of *Ephemera danica*, a large upwinged fly with three tails and upright hindwings.

Drawing 20:
Imago of *Baetis muticus*, a small upwinged fly with two tails and tiny oval hindwings.

Very large, large and medium-large flies

SECTION 1 Flies with three tails and large, upright hindwings (*Drawing 19*).

Group A (*page 44*): Large, upright but rather narrow hindwings without costal projections (*Drawing 4*).

Group B (*page 48*): Large, upright hindwings without costal projections, but wider than Group A (*Drawing 6*).

Group C (*page 50*): Large, upright hindwings with costal projections (*Drawing 3*), but wider than Group A (*Drawing 7*).

SECTION 2 Flies with two tails and large, upright hindwings with costal projections (*Drawing 3*).

Group D (*page 54*): The main wings are pale fawn and/or mottled.

Group E (*page 61*): The main wings are yellowish or dark grey.

Medium to very small flies

SECTION 3 Flies with two tails, pale-grey wings and tiny hindwings (*Drawing 20*).

Group F (*page 67*): Small, oval hindwings with small spur on top (*Drawing 8*).

Group G (*page 79*): Very tiny spur-shaped hindwings (*Drawing 10*).

SECTION 4 (*page 83*): Flies with two tails, no hindwings, and single intercalary veins (*Drawing 13*).

SECTION 5 (*page 89*): Very small flies with three tails, very broad main wings, and no hindwings (*Drawing 15*).

Localised flies

SECTION 6 (*page 91*): Localised or uncommon species which vary in size.

CHAPTER THREE

Nymphs of the Upwinged Flies

The nymphs of upwinged flies are similar to the adults less wings and long tails. The nymphs have three short tails and wing-cases along the top of the thorax which darken considerably with maturity. Most species of nymph in this Order swim up to hatch at the surface. A few of the larger species crawl ashore or up on to any convenient post, stone or other obstruction, where ecdysis takes place.

Nymphs of this Order vary slightly in shape according to species. These variations have evolved to suit the species' particular habitat, for they are adapted to widely differing conditions in various types of river, from the fast, freestone streams of the North to the placid chalk-streams of the South. As an example, the nymphs of the large **Mayfly** are adapted to live in the fine gravel or silt of rivers with a medium flow and are found only in this type of environment. They would find it impossible to live in fast-flowing rivers with stony beds. In contrast, nymphs of the **March Brown**, with their rather flattened bodies, are adapted to survive in this type of environment, where they cling to the underside of stones and boulders in fast-flowing water.

All these nymphs have tracheal gills along the sides of their abdomens. The gills of species living in fairly fast-flowing currents are generally smaller and less well-developed than those of species living in silt or burrowing in the river-bed, where there is little or no current. In these species, the gills are sometimes equipped with filaments and are capable of considerable muscular movement to provide constant circulation of water.

1 Mayfly Nymph (*E. danica*). A bottom-burrower

2 *Caenis* Nymphs. Silt-crawlers. The one at top is camouflaged with chalk particles

Although it is reasonably simple to identify the main families and some Genera in this Order, it is extremely difficult to distinguish one particular species from another, and as it serves no practical purpose from the fly-fisher's point of view, I shall not attempt to do so. However, it can sometimes be important to establish at least the Family by the shape of the nymph. The six main groups can be classified as: bottom-burrowers, silt-crawlers, moss creepers, stone-clingers, laboured swimmers, and agile darters.

3 Blue-winged Olive Nymph (*E. ignita*).
A moss-creeper

4 *Ecdyonurus* Nymph. A stone-clinger

Bottom-burrowers (1) The only nymphs in this
group are the various species of *Ephemera*, our
largest upwinged fly, the **Mayfly**. The nymphs are
large, robust creatures, cream-coloured with distinctive brown markings. They burrow into the silt
or fine gravel on the river-bed and live in the
tunnels so formed. They have a narrow head with a
pair of large mandibles which they use for excavat-
ing. The gills and filaments along the body are
prominent and are used probably not only to
circulate the water within their burrows but also to
attract small particles of food.

Silt-crawlers (2) These tiny nymphs live in the silt
or detritus at the bottom of lakes, ponds and rivers.
The group includes five species of *Caenis* and one

species of *Brachecercus*, but both nymphs and adults are difficult to tell apart. They are all commonly referred to as the **Angler's Curse** or **White Curse**. The nymphs are rather sluggish, but are adept at camouflage.

Moss-creepers (3) Within this group are only two species of the genus *Ephemerella*, the nymphs of *E. ignita* and *E. notata*, the **Blue-winged Olive** and the **Yellow Evening Dun**. They are similar to the *Baetidae* nymphs of the **Olives**, but are a little wider, more boldly marked, and appear slightly flattened. They seem to like decaying vegetation along the edges of gravel runs.

5 Sepia Nymph (*marginata*). A laboured swimmer

6 Large Summer Dun Nymph (*Siphlonurus spp*).
An agile darter

Stone-clingers (4) This group has several genera and many species, including *Rithrogena*,

Ecdyonurus and *Heptagenia*. These nymphs are well named, as they are able to cling to stones and boulders in even the strongest currents. Sturdy and almost as wide as they are long, they have a flattened appearance and vary in colour from various shades of green to dark-brown. Most species are boldly patterned in a darker shade. They favour the undersides of stones, where they can avoid the strongest flow. They often emerge on to the sides or downstream ends of stones as the light fades, presumably to feed on moss or algae, and it is then that trout take the opportunity to pick them off.

Laboured swimmers (5) The nymphs in this group are numerous and include the *Paraleptophlebia*, *Leptophlebia* and *Habrophlebia*, embracing the **Turkey Brown**, **Ditch Dun**, **Sepia Dun**, **Claret Dun** and **Purple Dun**. As the name suggests, these nymphs are rather lethargic and slow swimmers, but they are sturdy and a little wider than the agile darters. Most of them are dark-brown. Their gill-plates are long and slender.

7 Pond Olive Nymph (*dipterum*). An agile darter

Agile Darters (6) This is by far the largest group, embracing the Genera *Baetis*, *Centroptilum*, *Cloeon*, *Procloeon* and *Siphlonurus*. These include the various species of **Olives**, the **Spurwings**, the **Pond** and **Lake Olive**, and the **Large Summer Dun**, which is the largest of all the agile darters. The nymphs in this group are all accomplished

8 Large Dark Olive Nymph (*rhodani*). An agile darter

swimmers and live in heavy weed-growth. They are slim and mostly pale-green, although in strong sunlight they appear almost transparent. Their tails are strongly fringed with hairs to provide efficient propulsion.

Artificials

The nymphs in this Order are all similar, so it is not necessary to have individual patterns to represent the various types, although some specific patterns do represent a few of them. A **Pheasant Tail Nymph** in different sizes suffices for the darker-coloured species, and my own **PVC Nymph** in different sizes serves to match the lighter-coloured types. Colour, size and the manner in which a nymph is fished are the important factors. For trout feeding on the ascending or hatching nymphs, I would recommend a **GRHE Nymph** or **Collyer's Green** or **Brown Nymph**, either lightly weighted or unweighted, or a **Suspender Hatching Nymph**. Richard Walker's **Mayfly Nymph** is particularly effective for stillwater fishing, and Conrad Voss Bark's **Nymph** is a useful slow-sinker.

CHAPTER FOUR

Keys to Upwinged Duns and Spinners

Section 1 Flies with three tails and large, upright hindwings (*Drawing 19 page 36*).

Group A Duns with three tails and rather narrow, upright hindwings without costal projections (*Drawing 4 page 31*). **Turkey Brown**; **Purple Dun** (*page 92*).

TURKEY BROWN DUN/SPINNER
Paraleptophlebia submarginata

9 Turkey Brown Dun(female)

Habitat Running water.

Distribution/identification This species is widespread, from southern England to the Scottish Highlands, but hatches are sparse and of little value to the fly-fisher. The species has three tails, rather narrow, upright hindwings, a dark-brown body and fawn-mottled main wings.

Emergence In daytime in May and June, in ones or twos.

The dun The female has heavily-veined, fawn-

10 Turkey Brown Dun (male)

mottled wings, and a dark-brown body, tinged olive. The tails are dark grey-brown, and the legs dark olive-brown. The eyes are black, tinged with red. The male dun has wings and legs of similar colour, but the legs are darker brown and the body so dark that it appears almost black. The tails are also darker and the eyes are dull red.

Artificials No specific imitation, but an **August Dun** should be suitable.

11 Turkey Brown Spinner (female)   **12** Turkey Brown Spinner (male)

The spinner Like the dun, this spinner is of little value to the fisherman. It is similar to the spinner of the Blue-winged Olive. In fact, the two are difficult to tell apart. The female has transparent wings with pale-brown venation, a dark-brown body with pale-brown ringing, and dark-brown forelegs. The three tails are long, pale-brown and faintly ringed black. The male has transparent wings with pale-brown veining along the leading edges. The body is a translucent brown with the last three tail segments a darker brown. The legs are dark-brown and the three long tails are pale-brown and faintly ringed black. The male also has prominent dark-red eyes.

Artificials No specific imitation, but a **Sherry Spinner** or **Pheasant Tail Spinner** should suffice.

CLARET DUN/SPINNER
Leptophlebia vespertina

13 Claret Dun Nymph

14 Claret Dun (female)

Habitat Stillwater or, occasionally, slow-flowing water.

Distribution/identification This species is fairly easy to identify as it is the only upwinged fly to have upright hindwings that are a paler colour than

46

the main wings. It is fairly common on ponds and lakes and is widespread in Ireland. It may occasionally be seen on slow-flowing rivers, but it seems to prefer acid or peaty water. With its dark-grey wings and almost black body, it looks like a large Iron Blue.

The species is of most interest to stillwater fishermen, particularly in Ireland, where it is common on the big loughs. It is also quite common on lakes and reservoirs throughout England, North Wales and Scotland.

Emergence During the day from early May to early July.

The dun The female and male are similar. Both have dark-grey wings and hindwings of a much paler shade, particularly those of the female, which are pale buff. Each has a dark-brown, almost black, body, often with a distinct claret tinge. The legs and tails in both sexes are dark brown. The eyes of the male are prominent and are dark red-brown, compared with the smaller, almost black, eyes of the female.

Artificials A **Claret Dun** (J. R. Harris), an **Iron Blue Dun** (Russell), or a **Kite's Imperial**, size 14, should suffice. A **Mallard and Claret** is an excellent fly on stillwater.

15 Claret Spinner (female)   **16** Claret Spinner (male)

The spinner The female has transparent wings lightly-veined pale-brown and a brown body with a distinct claret tinge. The legs are pale brown as are the tails, which are ringed lightly in black. The male spinner is similar, but of little interest to the fly-fisher as the swarms occur, usually in early evening, well inland from water.

Artificials The **Claret Spinner** (J. R. Harris) is the only imitative pattern I know, although a **Pheasant Tail Spinner** would be a good alternative.

Section 1 Flies with three tails and large, upright hindwings (*Drawing 19 page 36*).

Group B Duns with three tails and wider, upright hindwings without costal projections (*Drawing 6 page 000*). **Claret Dun** and **Sepia Dun**.

SEPIA DUN/SPINNER
Leptophlebia marginata

17 Sepia Dun (female)

18 Sepia Dun (male)

Habitat Stillwater.

Distribution/identification Identification of this species is fairly easy as, apart from the previous two species, it is the only other upwinged fly with three tails that has such a dark-brown overall colour. Positive identification lies in the hindwings, as these are wider than in the previous two species (*Drawing 6*). Probably a little less common than the Claret Dun, it has not been recorded from Ireland. It is often a little larger than the Claret, but should not be confused as its wings are pale-fawn and appear very different to the Claret's dark-grey wings. A useful point of identification lies in the tails of the nymph, which are well spread, more so than in any other species. The three tails often cover an arc of nearly 180 degrees. This feature is noticeable also in some adults.

The Sepia Dun prefers slightly acid water and is often found in small, well-treed ponds and lakes. Although widely distributed in England and Scotland, it is rather uncommon.

Emergence During the middle of the day in April and early May, but hatches are usually rather sparse.

The dun The female and male are similar, with pale-fawn wings, heavily-veined brown, and a dark sepia-brown body. The legs are brown to olive-brown and the three tails are uniformly brown. The eyes of the male are dark-red-brown, compared to the smaller brown eyes of the female.

Artificials The **Sepia Dun** (Kite) is a good imitative pattern and **Terry's Terror** is a reasonable general pattern.

The Spinner The male and female are similar, with transparent wings, veined light-brown, and a dark-reddish brown body. The legs are brown to dark brown and the long tails are dark brown. The male's larger eyes are dark red-brown, tinged green, and its body is distinctly ringed in a straw colour. A feature which differentiates it from the Claret Spinner are the smokey-black patches along the top leading edges of the wings. The male swarms tend to form well away from the water's edge, so the male spinner is of little interest to fishermen.

Artificials I know of no special patterns, but a **Pheasant Tail Spinner** should be effective.

19 Sepia Spinner (female)   **20** Sepia Spinner (male)

Section 1 Flies with three tails and large upright hindwings (*Drawing 19 page 36*).

Group C Duns with three tails and large upright hindwings with costal projections (*Drawing 3 page 31*). **Mayfly· Blue-winged Olive** (*page 52*); **Yellow Evening Dun** (*page 91*); **Ditch Dun** (*page 93*).

MAYFLY (GREEN DRAKE/SPENT GNAT)
Ephemera danica, E. vulgata

21 Mayfly Dun (female) (*E. danica*)

Habitat Lakes, ponds, rivers.

Distribution/identification The Mayfly is by far the largest of the British upwinged flies. It has a wing-span of nearly 2 inches and can hardly be confused with any other species. It has three tails

22 Mayfly Dun (male) (*E. vulgata*).

and large upright hindwings. The Family includes three species, *E. danica*, *E. vulgata* and *E. lineata*, but the last is so rare that it can be discounted as far as the fisherman is concerned. The only difference between the other two species is in the markings on the underside of the body and the slightly darker overall colouration of *E. vulgata*. The male is generally much smaller than the female, and it is not uncommon to see specimens with a wing-span of only 1¼ inches.

E. danica, found in large lakes and faster-flowing streams, is the commoner of the two species and is widespread throughout the British Isles. *E. vulgata* is more likely to be found in slower-flowing rivers with muddy bottoms and smaller lakes and ponds. It is found only in southern England and parts of the Midlands.

Emergence The main hatch, exceedingly heavy in places, is usually confined to about three weeks, varying according to area from early May to early June. However, I have known specimens to hatch as late as August.

The dun The wings are heavily veined and grey, tinged yellowish-green. The body is ·creamy-yellow with constant brown markings. The tails are dark-grey to black, and the legs creamy-olive with black markings. The wings, tails and legs of the male are darker than those of the female and the body is often paler.

Artificials. Grey Wulff; Hackle-point Mayfly (Collyer); **Walker's Mayfly Dun; Poly-May Dun** (Goddard).

23 Mayfly Spinner (female)   **24** Mayfly Spinner (male)
(*E. danica*)   (*E. vulgata*)

The spinner (Spent Gnat) The wings are transparent and heavily veined brown with a few dark patches. The body is creamy-white with the last three segments brownish. Both male and female have extremely long, almost black, tails.
Artificials. Poly-May Spinner (Goddard); **Deerstalker** (Patterson).

BLUE-WINGED OLIVE DUN/SPINNER
Ephemerella ignita

25 Blue-winged Olive Dun (female)

Habitat Rivers; occasionally lakes.
Distribution/identification One of the most common of our upwinged flies, the B-WO is medium-

26 Blue-winged Olive Dun (male)

large and, with its blue-grey wings, upright hindwings and three tails, fairly easy to identify. In fact, with a little practice one can identify it at a fair distance, as its forewings slope back at a more acute angle than those of any other Olive. Trout often seem to feed on the B-WO to the exclusion of other species of Olive. The male tends to be a little smaller than the female.

The B-WO is found throughout the British Isles. It is abundant in rivers where the vegetation is thick, but is found also in small, stony streams and occasionally in lakes. It is a well-known species on many of our chalk-streams.

Emergence Hatches are often large, usually beginning in late evening towards the end of May and continuing to the end of the trout-fishing season. They tend to occur earlier, sometimes during the day, as the season progresses. After mating, the female spinners may be seen flying upstream in huge swarms, each fly with her large green egg-ball tucked beneath her tail. Favoured egg-laying sites for this species seem to be the faster, shallower stretches lined with gravel or heavy silt.

The dun The eyes of the female are dark greenish-black. The wings are a dark blue-grey and the body bright green-olive, darkening to a rusty-brown-olive as the season progresses. The three tails are pale grey, ringed dark brown. The male has red eyes and its body varies from orange-brown to olive-brown. The tail segment is often yellowish.

Artificials. B-WO Dun (Jacques); **B-WO Dun** (Nice); **B-WO Dun** (Walker); **Orange Quill**.

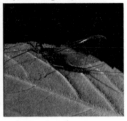

27 Sherry Spinner   **28** Blue-Winged Olive
(B-WO female)   Spinner (male)

The spinner The eyes of the female are greenish-brown and the wings are transparent with pale-brown veins. The body varies from olive-brown to a deep sherry-red, hence the popular name, the Sherry Spinner. The three tails are olive-grey, faintly ringed brown. The male has bright red eyes, and its body is dark brown-red but seldom attains the deep sherry-red colour of the female.
Artificials. Sherry Spinner (Lunn); **Pheasant Tail Spinner**.

Section 2 Flies with only two tails and large, upright hindwings with costal projections (*Drawing 3 page 31*).
Group D Duns with two tails and large upright hindwings with costal projections (*Drawing 3 page 31*) and pale fawn sometimes mottled wings, **Autumn Dun**; **Large Brook Dun** (*page 57*); **March Brown** (*page 59*); **Late March Brown** (*page 95*); **Large Green Dun** (*page 94*).

AUTUMN DUN/SPINNER
Ecdyonurus dispar

Habitat Stony rivers and stony shores of lakes.
Distribution/identification This species was for many years confused with the March Brown as the two are of similar size and appearance apart from the colour of the wings. However, this species is

29 Autumn Dun Nymph

30 Autumn Dun (male)

likely to be encountered only in autumn (hence its colloquial name) and there should be no confusion. It is of interest to both river and stillwater fly-fishers, as the flat, stone-clinging nymphs, unlike most others in the family, are able to live in water with little or no flow. The one other species that could be mistaken for this one is the Late March Brown, but this is rather scarce and has strongly-mottled wings, so confusion should not arise.

The species favours stony or boulder-strewn rivers as well as the shores of stony lakes. It is fairly common and is found in the West Country, parts of Wales, in the North of England, and in some areas of Scotland. Specimens have been recorded also in the extreme north of Ireland.

Emergence The duns emerge during the day and the spinners may be seen in early evening. The species occurs from July to early October, but the peak hatches are during August and September.

The dun The male and female have similar wings, uniformly grey with a yellowish tinge and prominent blackish veins. In some lights they seem to be a fawn colour (*Drawing 16 page 34*). The tails are dark grey and the legs dark brown-olive. The forelegs are very long. The body of the female is brownish-olive with dark-brown patches or bands along the sides. These patches are not so prominent on the body of the male, which is a more reddish-brown colour. The eyes of the female are dark brown, while those of the male are more prominent and are greenish-brown.

Artificials. August Dun (Woolley), although any of the many **March Brown** patterns should be effective.

31 Autumn Spinner
(female)

32 Autumn Spinner
(male)

The spinner The Autumn Spinner is so similar to the spinner of the Late March Brown that it is all but impossible to distinguish them. However, the body of the male Autumn Spinner is often bright red-brown, though it is of doubtful value to the angler as it is seldom seen on the water in quantity. The male and female are similar, with transparent wings with heavy brown veining, long, dark-brown tails, and brownish legs. The eyes of both are similar to those of the duns. The body of the female is red-brown, while that of the male is often bright red-brown with blackish joins to the segments.

Artificials A large **Red Spinner** or **Pheasant Tail Spinner**.

LARGE BROOK DUN/SPINNER

Ecdyonurus torrentis

33 Large Brook Dun (female)

34 Large Brook Dun (male)

Habitat Stony streams and rivers.

Distribution/identification This species was not acknowledged by fly-fishermen until comparatively recently, as it is very similar to the March Brown or the Late March Brown. The dun is of doubtful value anyway, as the nymph is a stone-clinger that crawls towards the shore and emerges above the surface via stones or posts. The dun is therefore seldom available to the trout.

This species, which prefers stony streams or rivers, is widespread, but not common. It is found throughout the British Isles apart from Ireland, where it has been recorded only in the far north.

Emergence Hatches tend to be sparse and occur during the day or early evening from late March to July.

The dun The female is a handsome fly and once identified will not be forgotten. It is much larger than the male, but otherwise the sexes are similar. The wings are pale fawn, mottled with black transverse bands (*Drawing 18 page 34*) and the leading edges have a strong yellowish tinge. The body is olive-brown while the sides of the body segments are red-brown, giving a banded appearance. The underbody, or venter, is a distinct purple. The legs are dark olive-brown, although those of the female sometimes have patches of purple. The tails are long and purple-brown.

Artificials No specific pattern. A large **Pheasant Tail** is suggested.

35 Large Brook Spinner (female)   **36** Large Brook Spinner (male)

The spinner Due to its large size, the Large Brook Spinner makes a meal for any trout. The female, in common with several other species, is often referred to as the Large Red Spinner. The spinners of both sexes are similar. They have transparent wings with dark-brown to black veining and yellowish leading edges. Their bodies are dark olive-brown, banded with red to purple-brown, while their venters are purple. The legs of the female are dark to pale brown and those of the male, dark olive-brown. The tails are purple-brown and very long on the male. The female lays her eggs on the water surface in batches by dipping. The males usually swarm either over the water or along the shoreline.

Artificials No known pattern. A **Large Red Spinner** or **Pheasant Tail Spinner** should suffice.

MARCH BROWN DUN/SPINNER
Rithrogena germanica

37 March Brown Dun (female)

38 March Brown Dun(male)

Habitat Larger stony rivers.

Distribution/identification The species is found in larger rivers with stony or boulder-strewn beds throughout Britain apart from southern England, though it is not common. It is scarce in Ireland.

The nymph is of the flattened stone-clinging type, but it does hatch in open water, often making several exploratory trips to the surface before hatching. The species is similar to the four members of the *Ecdyonurus* genera. There is little difference between male and female.

Emergence Hatches, where they do occur, are often on a grand scale during the middle of the day in March, April and early May. Most trout seem to feed on the nymphs just below the surface as they are about to emerge.

The dun The fawn wings are strongly mottled black, but a useful identification feature is the distinctive clear patch in the middle which is devoid of cross-veins. The body is dark, almost mahogany-brown, and the joints between the body segments are a distinctive straw colour. The legs are brown to pale brown, while the tails are dark brown. The eyes in both sexes are green with a black horizontal bar across the centre.

Artificials The artificial **March Brown** is one of our oldest angling flies. Several of the many dressings available are close to those in use 200 years ago. When trout are reluctant to take duns on the surface, a **March Brown Spider** or a **Partridge and Orange** fished just sub-surface may succeed.

39 March Brown Spinner (female)   **40** March Brown Spinner (male)

The spinner This spinner is of doubtful value to the fisherman as it is seldom seen on the surface in any quantity. Apart from its transparent wings, with brown veining, the colours of the spinner are similar to those of the dun, except that its body has a little more red in it. There is little difference between male and female. Flies of the *Rithrogena* genus have a distinctive dark oval spot in the centre of each femur joint of their legs. The male spinners swarm over water and the females oviposit by dipping.

Artificials No specific pattern. A large **Pheasant Tail Spinner** is suggested.

Section 2 Flies with two tails and large, upright hindwings with costal projections (*Drawing 3 page 31*)

Group E Duns with only two tails and large, upright hindwings with costal projections (*Drawing 3 page 31*), but with yellow or dark-grey wings. **Large Summer Dun**, **Yellow May Dun** (*page 63*), **Olive Upright** (*page 65*), and **Dusky Yellowstreak** (*page 96*).

LARGE SUMMER DUN/SPINNER
Siphlonurus spp

41 Large Summer Dun (female)

42 Large Summer Dun (male)

Habitat Lakes and slow-flowing rivers.
Distribution/identification Flies of this genus are simple to identify due to their large size. They are almost as large as the Mayfly (Green Drake), but completely different in appearance. The three species, *S. alternatus*, *S. armatus* and *S. lacustris*, are rather uncommon apart from *S. lacustris*, which

is fairly common in the North of England. Trout seem wary of them where hatches are sparse, probably due to their large size.

The nymphs are large and slim and belong to the group known as agile darters. They are reputed to crawl ashore to hatch above the waterline, but I doubt that this applies to all three species. I have watched *S. armatus* hatching in open water at Darwell Reservoir in Sussex, one of the few locations I know in the south of England where these large duns are to be seen.

The three species are found in lakes and in many Scottish lochs, as well as slow-flowing rivers. They are locally quite common in Scotland.

Emergence During the day from June to late August.

The dun An extremely handsome fly. The three species are similar apart from a slight variation in the colour of the wings, which vary from grey to brownish-grey through to greenish-grey. Their bodies are olive-brown with variable dark brown markings while their legs and tails are olive-brown. There is little difference between males and females.

Artificials. Large Summer Dun (Price) or a good general pattern such as a **Grey Wulff**.

The spinner The female is called the Great Red Spinner in some areas. The males swarm over water and the females dip down over water to release their eggs in one mass. There is little difference between male and female. They have transparent wings with brown venation and their bodies are olive-brown, tending in the female at least, to darken to a red-brown with age.

Artificials. Large Summer Spinner (Price).

43 Large Summer Spinner (female)   **44** Large Summer Spinner (male)

YELLOW MAY DUN/SPINNER
Heptagenia sulphurea

45 Yellow May Dun (female)

46 Yellow May Dun (male)

Habitat Rivers and some calcareous lakes.
Distribution/identification This is one of the easiest of the upwinged flies to identify, with its two grey tails and overall colour of bright sulphur-

yellow. The only species with which it might be confused is the Yellow Evening Dun, but this is a much paler yellow and has three tails. The trout are reputed to dislike the Yellow May Dun, and it is of doubtful interest to the fly-fisher. I have only rarely seen one taken by a trout, but this may be at least partly due to the fact that emergence is usually sparse.

The nymph is slightly flattened and is a stone-clinger. Unlike most nymphs in this group, it emerges at the surface in open water.

The Yellow May Dun is usually found in slower-flowing rivers and occasionally in lakes, and it is often seen on the chalk-streams. It is a common and widespread species throughout the British Isles and in Ireland, where it is often known as the Yellow Hawk.

Emergence During day and early evening throughout the summer, but hatches are usually sparse.

The dun While the overall colour of the wings, body and legs is bright sulphur-yellow, the venation on the wings is pale yellow-brown. The feet and tails are grey. The only noticeable difference between female and male is that the latter has large and distinctive blue eyes.

Artificials. Yellow May Dun (Price); **Yellow May Dun** (Roberts).

47 Yellow May Spinner (female)   **48** Yellow May Spinner (male)

The spinner I have seen trout taking this spinner, but the falls are always so sparse that it can almost be discounted. It is a handsome fly, particularly the male with its bright golden-brown body and bright-blue eyes. The transparent wings are veined dark brown and the leading edges are often a smoky-grey colour. The long forelegs are also golden-brown. The female is similar, but has smaller pale-blue eyes. The wings are pale yellow along the leading edges, while the legs are more of an olive colour. Swarms of male spinners are unlikely to be seen as they usually occur in such small numbers. The females lay their eggs on the water surface by dipping.

Artificials. Lunn's Yellow Boy dressed on a large hook.

OLIVE UPRIGHT DUN/SPINNER
Rithrogena semicolorata

49 Olive Upright Dun (female)

50 Olive Upright Dun (male)

Habitat Stony streams and rivers.

Distribution/identification Although this is one of the commonest and most widespread of the upwinged flies, one authority on the *Ephemeroptera* has stated that it has never been recorded from southern or eastern England. However, I did see quite a heavy hatch of this species several years ago over a two-week period on the lower beat of the famous Abbots Barton fishery of the Itchen.

The nymph is similar to the nymph of the Yellow May Dun and is also a stone-clinger, being slightly flattened. It emerges at the surface in open water. Like the March Brown, the dun has a distinct dark oval mark in the middle of each top leg section (femora), which is a useful point of identification. The female dun is similar to the Blue-winged Olive, apart from the latter's three tails, although it is easy to confuse the two.

Emergence This species sometimes emerges in early morning, but more normally from early afternoon through almost to dusk. It occurs throughout the summer, but the peak hatches are from mid-May to mid-July.

The dun The female has dark-blue-grey wings and the trailing edges of the hindwings are buff-coloured. The body is grey-olive-brown, ringed olive, and the legs and tails of both sexes are pale olive-brown to grey-brown. The wings of the male are also dark-blue-grey, while the body is dark-grey-olive, ringed olive, and the eyes are dark olive, almost black. The eyes of the female are dull green with a brown bar across the centre. The side of the thorax is a distinctive orange colour in both sexes.

Artificials The only imitative pattern I know is the **HPB** (Evans). Good general patterns are **Kite's Imperial** or my own **Super Grizzly**.

The spinner The popular name for this spinner in areas where it is common is Yellow Upright. Although this species is unfamiliar to fly-fishers in the South, both dun and spinner are important in

51 Yellow Upright Spinner
(female)

52 Yellow Upright Spinner
(male)

other areas. There is little difference between male and female. They have olive-yellow eyes with a dark bar across the centre, and the transparent wings are lightly-veined brown, while the lower halves are often a smoky-bronze colour. Their bodies are brown to yellow-olive and they have pale-olive-grey legs. The tails of the male are grey-buff, while those of the female are pale-buff faintly ringed red. The male swarms are seen over water and the females oviposit just below the surface via any convenient stone or other projection from the water.

Artificials No known pattern, but a **Lunn's Yellow Boy** (ungreased) should prove effective.

Section 3 Flies with two tails and very small hindwings.

Group F Duns with two tails and very small, oval-shaped hindwings with tiny spurs (*Drawing 8 page 32*) and double intercalary veins along trailing edges of the main wings (*Drawing 12 page 33*). **Large Dark Olive**; **Medium Olive** (*page 70*); **Small Dark Olive** (*page 72*); **Pale Watery** (*page 74*); and **Iron Blue** (*page 76*).

LARGE DARK OLIVE DUN/SPINNER
Baetis rhodani

Habitat Streams and rivers.
Distribution/identification This is one of the earliest upwinged flies to appear on the chalk-streams of southern England. An olive-bodied,

53 Large Dark Olive Dun (female)

54 Large Dark Olive Dun (male)

medium-large fly with grey wings seen on the water in March or April is almost certainly this species. It is considerably larger than most other olives. A similar species, *Baetis atrebatinus*, the Dark Dun, hatches a little later in the season (the only difference between the two is that the latter does not have the tiny spur on the oval hindwing shown in *Drawing 9 page 32*), but is rare and can more or less be discounted.

The Large Dark Olive nymph is one of the agile darters and lives among the vegetation of weedy rivers with a good flow. It emerges at the surface in open water.

The Large Dark Olive seems to have a greater tolerance of varying water conditions than any other olive. It is the commonest and most abundant of the olives and is found all over the British Isles.

Emergence Hatches occur during the day from October to early May and are often prolific.

The dun Both sexes have pale-grey wings with pale-brown veins, dark-olive-brown to green bodies, pale-green or olive legs with black feet, and dull-grey tails. The eyes of the female are greenish, while the larger eyes of the male are dull brick-red. The last segment of the body of the male is a lighter yellow-olive.

Artificials. GRHE (winged); **Kite's Imperial**; **USD Dun**; **Funnel Dun**; **Rough Olive** (Skues); **Beacon Beige**; or my own **Super Grizzly**.

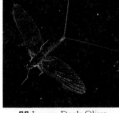 

55 Large Dark Olive Spinner (female)   **56** Large Dark Olive Spinner (male)

The spinner Large Dark Olive Spinners are of doubtful value to fly-fishers as they are seldom seen on the water in sufficient quantities. This is because the species is an early-season one and our spring weather is seldom warm enough in the evening to favour swarming, so mating takes place during the day as and when the opportunity occurs. The female spinner, sometimes known as the Red Spinner, often crawls underwater to a considerable depth to deposit her eggs. Both male and female have transparent wings with brown veins. Their legs are dark-olive-grey with darker feet and they have grey tails ringed red-brown. The female has a reddish-brown body with pale-olive rings and dark-brown eyes. The body of the male is pale-olive, tinged brown in places, and the last three segments are orange-brown. Both have prominent dark-red eyes.

Artificials. Lunn's Particular or a **Red Spinner**.

MEDIUM OLIVE DUN/SPINNER
Baetis vernus, B. tenax and *B. buceratus*

57 Medium Olive Dun (female)

58 Medium Olive Dun (male)

Habitat Streams and rivers.

Distribution/identification This is an important fly on the chalk-streams, but there is no reliable method of distinguishing between the first two species. *B. tenax* seems to prefer small, stony streams at higher altitudes and is common in the North, while *B. vernus* inhabits slower-flowing, weedy rivers and is more common in the South. *B. buceratus* is similar, but rather rare and can be discounted. They are similar to the small spur-wings, but these have tiny spur-shaped hindwings as opposed to the small oval-shaped hindwings of the Medium Olive.

All the Olives in this group have double intercalary veins along the trailing edges of the main wings (*Drawing 12 page 33*) as opposed to the single intercalary veins (*Drawing 13 page 33*) of flies in the remaining groups. A low-power magnifying glass will show these. The nymphs are agile darters and cling to stones or weed. Emergence is at surface in open water.

Both *B. vernus* and *B. tenax* are widespread in England and Scotland, but neither has been recorded in Wales or Ireland.

Emergence During the day or early evening throughout the summer, with a peak in May and June. Hatches are often heavy.

The dun The male has dull-grey wings with tinges of golden-olive along the veins. The body is dark grey to medium-olive and the underpart of the last segment is yellow-olive. The large compound eyes are dull red-brown. The wings of the female are dull grey with light-brown veining and the body is brown to medium-olive. The eyes are dull yellow-green.

Artificials. GRHE (winged); **Kite's Imperial**; **Beacon Beige**; **USD Dun**; **Super Grizzly**; and **Greenwell's Glory**.

59 Medium Olive Spinner (female) **60** Medium Olive Spinner (male)

The spinner The Medium Olive Spinner and the spinners of the following olive species are important to fly-fishers. This species is largely responsible for the season's first serious evening rises towards the middle of May. Swarms of male spinners form in early evenings over the river banks and the females crawl underwater via posts, piers of bridges, or weed-stems protruding above the water to lay their eggs often at a considerable depth. The spinners die, float to the surface and then drift downstream just below the surface film. Artificials to represent them should be fished in or just below the film. Both male and female spinners have transparent wings with light-brown veins, grey-olive legs and long off-white tails. The body of the male is usually grey-olive, with the last three segments red-brown, and the eyes are brown.

Artificials. Pheasant Tail; Lunn's Particular; Red Spinner; USD Poly Spinner; and **Sunk Spinner** (Patterson).

SMALL DARK OLIVE DUN/SPINNER
Baetis scambus

61 Small Dark Olive Dun (female)

62 Small Dark Olive Dun (male)

Habitat Streams and rivers.

Distribution/identification Another important fly on the chalk-streams, and the sheet anchor of the dry-fly fisherman from mid-summer onwards. It is the smallest of the upwinged flies. In some areas it is still referred to as the July Dun. The size of the chosen artificial is of utmost importance and should be no larger than size 16, and preferably an 18.

The nymph is again one of the agile darters and is found either in weed or among gravel or sand on the river-bed.

The species favours alkaline water and occurs in parts of the West Country, the South of England, eastern Wales and as far north as Yorkshire and parts of southern Scotland. It has not been recorded in Ireland.

Emergence At the surface in open water. Hatches are often substantial and prolonged from mid-day until late evening. They occur from June until November, with a peak in July and August.

The dun The only difference between the male and female is the colour of the eyes: dull-orange-red in the male; almost black in the female. The wings are medium to dark grey and the body grey-olive with the last two segments yellowish. The legs are pale yellow-olive and the feet black, but as the season progresses the top joints of the legs become a distinct yellow. The tails are pale grey.

Artificials. July Dun (Skues); **Last Hope** (dark) (Goddard); **Kite's Imperial**; **GRHE** (winged); **Funnel Dun** (Patterson); and **USD Dun**.

63 Small Dark Olive Spinner (female)

64 Small Dark Olive Spinner (male)

The spinner The female is generally referred to as the Small Red Spinner. The males usually swarm over the banks or in the shelter of adjacent trees or bushes. The females usually crawl underwater to lay their eggs and eventually die. Spent and dying spinners are swept downstream and then up to the

73

surface where they drift down beneath the surface film. The chosen artificial should be fished likewise.

Both male and female have olive-brown legs and greyish-white tails, but the wings of the male are transparent and its body is a translucent cream, with the last three segments an opaque orange-brown. The eyes of the male are bright orange-red. The wings of the female are also transparent, but the veins are darker and more apparent, and the body varies from dark brown to deep red-brown with age. The eyes of the female are black.

Artificials. Pheasant Tail; **Red Spinner**; **USD Poly Spinner**; and **Sunk Spinner** (Patterson).

PALE WATERY
Baetis fuscatus

65 Pale Watery Dun(female)

66 Pale Watery Dun (male)

Habitat Streams and rivers.
Distribution/identification The female of this spe-

cies is one of the most difficult of the upwinged flies to identify. While it is designated as "small", it varies in size more than any other olive. It may be almost as large as a Medium Olive or almost as small as a small Dark Olive. At times it is all but impossible to separate the female duns of these three species. But the Pale Watery is another common species on the chalk-streams.

The nymph is again an agile darter. Two other species, the Small Spurwing and the Large Spurwing, were formerly referred to as Pale Wateries, but they have now been reclassified.

The Pale Watery is reputed to prefer slightly more calcareous water than the previous species, but is found in the same type of habitat. It is common and widespread in the South of England, parts of Wales, and as far north as Yorkshire. It has not been recorded in Ireland.

Emergence At the surface in open water during the day from May to October. Hatches are sometimes heavy.

The dun The male and female duns are similar, having pale-grey wings, lightly-veined pale brown, and distinctive pale-watery-olive bodies with the last two segments pale yellow. These colours can often assist in their identification. Their legs are pale olive, their feet dark grey, and their tails grey. The eyes of the female are yellow-green, while those of the male are bright orange-yellow. This feature, too, is of great assistance in identification, as in only one other species of upwinged fly does the male have such distinctive yellow eyes, and that is the Pale Evening Dun.

Artificials. Last Hope (light) (Goddard); **Little Marryat**; **Pale Watery Dun** (Walker); and, on fast waters, **Dogsbody**.

The spinner The female is commonly known as the Golden Spinner, due to its distinctive body colour. It is not so important to the fly-fisher as most others in this group, as it is seldom seen in large numbers and often falls spent earlier in the

67 Pale Watery Spinner (female)   **68** Pale Watery Spinner (male)

evening than most. However, trout seem some-times to prefer it, so it is wise to carry a suitable artificial.

The males often swarm well away from the banks and the females are reputed to lay their eggs underwater, as do other members of this genus, but I have not seen this. The male spinner has distinctive orange-yellow eyes, transparent wings, and a translucent creamy-white body with the last three segments orange-brown. The legs are also translucent white with touches of olive. Both male and female have long greyish-white tails. The female spinner also has translucent wings, but its body is a distinctive golden-olive, with the last three segments a slightly darker shade. The legs are pale olive-brown and the eyes are dark brown.

Artificials. Lunn's Yellow Boy; Pale Watery (Skues).

IRON BLUE DUN/SPINNER
Baetis niger and *B. muticus*

Habitat Streams and rivers.
Distribution/identification These two species are so similar that it is impossible to tell them apart without a microscope. *B. niger* prefers weedy rivers and is the species we are so familiar with on our chalk-streams, while *B. muticus* is found in fast-flowing, stony rivers. Legend is that trout have an inordinate liking for this little fly and that it

69 Iron Blue Dun (female)

70 Iron Blue Dun (male)

hatches only on wet, windy days. But while there is a great deal of truth in both points, I have also seen countless hatches in excellent conditions. It is an easy species to identify as it is the only small upwinged fly that has such an overall dark colouration.

The nymphs belong to the agile darter group.

B. niger is common in the Midlands and the South, while *B. muticus* is widespread throughout the British Isles.

Emergence At the surface in open water during the day. Hatches are sometimes prolific (but seldom regular) throughout the summer, with peaks in May and September.

The dun There is little difference between male and female apart from the colour and size of the eyes, which are dull red-brown in the male and dull yellow-green in the female. Their wings are dull grey-blue and their bodies dark brown tinged olive. The legs are pale to dark olive-brown and the tails are dark grey.

Artificials. Iron Blue (Russell); **Blue Upright** (Austin); **Otter Ruby** (Nice); **Iron Blue Quill**.

71 Iron Blue (Claret) Spinner (female)

72 Iron Blue (Jenny) Spinner (male)

The spinner The female spinner is often called the Little Claret Spinner, from the colour of its body. The male, an extremely handsome little fly, is often referred to as the Jenny Spinner. While hatches of duns are sometimes heavy and prolonged, falls of spinners are often sparse. However, when they do occur, it is important to have a good imitative pattern.

The Iron Blue is not an evening fly. Male spinners tend to swarm during the day, and mating and egg-laying consequently also often take place during the day. The females, like most others in this group, crawl underwater to lay their eggs and the dying spinners are most likely to be found drifting down with the current just beneath the surface film. Both sexes have transparent wings and pale-grey legs and tails. The body of the female is dark claret-brown, while that of the male is a translucent pearly-white, with the last three segments dark orange-brown.

Artificials. Houghton Ruby (Lunn); **Pheasant Tail Spinner** (small).

Section 3 Flies with two tails and very small hindwings.

Group G Duns with two tails and very tiny spur-shaped hindwings (*Drawing 10 page 33*) and single intercalary veins along trailing edges of main wing (*Drawing 13 page 33*). **Small Spurwing**; **Large Spurwing** (*page 81*).

SMALL SPURWING DUN/SPINNER
Centroptilum luteolum

73 Small Spurwing Dun (female)

74 Small Spurwing Dun (male)

Habitat Rivers and lakes.

Distribution/identification Common in many rivers, the Small Spurwing is also fairly abundant in lakes and is of value to the stillwater fly-fisher. Its size varies tremendously, some specimens being as large as a Medium Olive, others as small as a Pale Watery, so it is not easy to separate the three species. This and the following species used to be classed with the Pale Wateries, but they are now

79

generally accepted under their new names, due largely to the late Major Oliver Kite. It used also to be known as **Little Sky Blue**. The nymph is again one of the agile darters, living on weed.

Any doubt over their identification should be dispelled by looking at the hindwings with a low-power glass. The Small and Large Spurwings are the only two upwinged flies to have such tiny spur-shaped hindwings.

Although the Small Spurwing prefers alkaline water, and is common on the chalk-streams, it is widespread and is found in weedy or sandy locations as well as around exposed lake shores throughout the British Isles.

Emergence At the surface in open water during the day from early May through to September.

The dun The eyes of the male are bright orange-red, the body is pale olive-grey, and the legs are brown-olive with grey feet. The female has pale-green eyes, a pale-watery, brown-olive body and pale-olive legs with grey feet. The wings of both vary from pale grey to blue-grey. Their tails are also grey.

Artificials. Little Marryat; **Last Hope** (light); **Grey Duster**; and perhaps **Dogsbody** on fast water.

 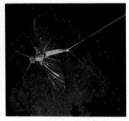

75 Small Spurwing (Little Amber) Spinner (female)   **76** Small Spurwing Spinner (male)

The spinner This is an early-season species and its spinners are often responsible for evening rises as weather and water warm up towards the end of May. The males swarm close to the water and are often blown on to the surface, where the trout take them readily. It is one of the few species of which it pays to have a copy of the male spinner. The females lay their eggs by dipping and releasing a few at a time.

The male is similar to the Pale Watery, but can be quickly distinguished by its bright orange-red eyes (the eyes of the Pale Watery are yellow). It has a translucent watery-white body, with the last three segments pale orange-brown, and pale-olive legs. The female, commonly called the Little Amber Spinner, has dark-brown eyes and, when fully spent, the top half of the body is a lovely pale-amber colour, ringed cream. The underbody is pale creamy-yellow and the legs pale olive-brown. It is a most distinctive-looking spinner and, once correctly identified, is unlikely to be forgotten.

Artificials. Lunn's Yellow Boy; **Tup's Indispensable**; **Lunn's Particular**; or a **Pale Watery Spinner** to represent the male.

LARGE SPURWING DUN/SPINNER
Centroptilum pennulatum

77 Large Spurwing Dun (female)

Habitat Slow-flowing rivers and streams.
Distribution/identification A rather uncommon medium-large species which can be positively identified by its small, spur-shaped hindwings. These are rounded at the apex as opposed to those of the Small Spurwing, which are pointed (*Drawings 10 and 11 page 33*). While hatches are seldom

78 Large Spurwing Dun (male)

large, trout seem to have a particular liking for this fly. I have often seen fish feeding on them in preference to other species. With practice, it can often be identified on sight from the colour combination of dark-grey-blue wings and light-olive-grey body. It is the only upwinged fly I know which is often to be seen with its main wings spread well apart.

The species is rather localised, but can be seen throughout the British Isles, though not in Ireland.

Emergence Hatches are rarely consistent from year to year and are seldom large. Although the fly may be seen on the wing from May to October, June is the favoured month.

The dun The two tails are grey, the legs olive with greyish feet, and the wings dark grey-blue. The male has dull-orange eyes and a pale-olive-brown body with the last three segments an amber colour. The female has yellow-green eyes and a pale-olive to creamy-grey body.

Artificials. Tup's Indispensable; **Pale Watery Dun** (Walker).

The spinner The female is sometimes known as the Large Amber Spinner, and its overall colour is similar to that of the Small Amber Spinner. Both male and female are exceedingly handsome and seem to be appreciated by the trout. Unfortunately, falls seem to be declining. Both male and female have transparent wings, long pale-grey tails and pale-olive-grey legs. The male has bright-orange eyes while its body is translucent white, ringed

79 Large Spurwing
Spinner (female)

80 Large Spurwing
Spinner (male)

pale red, with the last three segments dark amber.
The female has dark-yellow-green eyes and the
body is pale-olive, flecked with deep rich amber.
Male spinners are only occasionally seen on the
water.

**Artificials. Lunn's Yellow Boy; Pale Watery
Spinner** (Skues).

Section 4 Duns with only two tails, no hindwings
and single intercalary veins along trailing edges of
main wing (*Drawing 13 page 33*). **Pond Olive;
Lake Olive** (*page 86*); **Pale Evening Dun** (*page
88*).

POND OLIVE DUN/SPINNER
Cloeon dipterum

81 Pond Olive Dun (female)

Habitat Slow rivers; ponds and lakes.
Distribution/identification This species is of great
interest to the stillwater fly-fisher, as it is one of the
most important upwinged flies on those ponds,

82 Pond Olive Dun (male)

reservoirs and lakes where it occurs. Although the duns of this and the Lake Olive are similar, the females (dun and spinner) can be quickly identified by two parallel red lines which traverse the length of the underbody.

Identification of the males of the two species can usually be established by the eyes. Those of the Pond Olive have two faint red parallel lines across the centre. Examination of the top leading edges of the main wings of the two species with a low-power glass will show that the Pond Olive has only three to five small cross-veins (*Drawing 15 page 34*), while the Lake Olive has nine to eleven (*Drawing 14 page 34*). The size of the female varies tremendously in the early summer, from medium to medium-large.

The Pond Olive is common and widespread in northern and south-east England.

Emergence During the day throughout the summer, with peaks in June, July and September.

The dun The male has dull-orange-brown eyes with two faint red lines across the centre. The wings are pale grey and the body grey-olive, with the last three segments grey-brown. The legs are pale-watery white with faint reddish marks on top of the forelegs. The female has dull-green eyes with two faint red lines across centre, and her body is dark brownish-olive, often streaked red. The legs are pale-watery olive and the top of the forelegs are suffused reddish. Both have pale-grey tails, heavily ringed dark brown as opposed to the pale unringed tails of the Lake Olive. The dun quickly becomes airborne, so an emerging pattern is often desirable.

Artificials. Pond Olive Dun (Price); **Greenwell's Glory**; **Olive Quill**; **GRHE**.

83 Pond Olive (Apricot) Spinner (female)   **84** Pond Olive Spinner (male)

The spinner The female is unique among the upwinged flies as the eggs develop and (after about 14 days) hatch within her body. The larvae are then released on to the water a few at a time and swim to the bottom. This takes place in the late evening or at night, so it is not unusual to find lake margins littererd with dead and dying spinners in early morning, with the trout rising to them for two or three hours after sunrise.

The popular name for this spinner is Apricot, and once one has been identified, it will never be confused with any other. The wings of the female are transparent with red-brown veining, and the whole of the leading edge is a distinctive bronze-yellow. The body varies from apricot streaked with red to red-brown, tinged dark yellow, with two parallel red lines along the underbody. The legs are bright olive-green and the forelegs are often ringed in red. The eyes are black.

The male has orange-red eyes with two faint parallel red lines and its wings are transparent with distinctive brown veins along the leading edges. The body is dull translucent cream with the last three segments dark brown. The legs are pale grey-white, and the tails are brown-ringed.

Artificials. Pond Olive Spinner (Goddard); **Lunn's Yellow Boy**.

LAKE OLIVE DUN/SPINNER
Cloeon simile

85 Lake Olive Dun (female)

86 Lake Olive Dun (male)

Habitat Lakes and slow rivers.

Distribution/identification Although it is similar to the previous species, the Lake Olive should not be confused with the Pond Olive. It has a much drabber appearance and its tails are dark grey as opposed to the pale-grey, distinctly brown-ringed tails of the Pond Olive. Any doubt may be solved by examining the top leading edges of the main wings with a low-power glass. The Pond Olive has three to five small cross-veins (*Drawing 15 page 34*), while the Lake Olive has nine to eleven (*Drawing 14 page 34*). The nymph of the latter, one of the agile darters, is likely to be found at greater depths than the former.

The Lake Olive is common and widespread, being found all over the British Isles. It prefers deeper water.

Emergence During the day throughout the summer, with peaks in May and June and again in August and September. The dun becomes airborne very quickly.

The dun The male and female are similar, with smoky-grey wings with yellowish venation along the leading edges. Their bodies are pale reddish to grey-brown, with pale ringing, and they have olive-green legs with black feet. The tails are dark grey. The eyes of the male are olive-brown, while those of the female are olive with brown spots.
Artificials. Lake Olive Dun (C. F. Walker); **Greenwell's Glory**; **GRHE**; **Rough Olive**.

 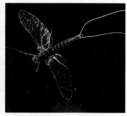

87 Lake Olive Spinner (female) **88** Lake Olive Spinner (male)

The spinner With the species' preference for deep water, the spinners are often found over a wide area and are more common than the Pond Olive on large lakes. During a period of good hatches, reasonable falls of spent female spinners are likely during early evening, particularly on warm, still evenings.

The female can be distinguished from the Pond Olive Spinner as it has transparent wings with only faint touches of yellow along the leading edges and deep-chestnut-brown body. The legs are pale olive-yellow, the feet black, and the tails white, faintly ringed red (see also **95**). The male has similar wings, but the body is pale brown-olive, with the last three segments deep red-brown. The legs are pale yellow, the feet black, and the tails long and white, faintly ringed red. The eyes of both are yellow to olive-green.
Artificials. Lunn's Particular; Pheasant Tail Spinner.

PALE EVENING DUN/SPINNER
Procleon bifidum

89 Pale Evening Dun (female)

90 Pale Evening Spinner (female)

Habitat Slow rivers and streams.

While this species is often locally abundant, it is rather uncommon. Nevertheless, it is found all over the British Isles. The spinners are of doubtful value as they are rarely seen and probably oviposit after dark.

The nymph is an agile darter and is found in weed.

Emergence At the surface in open water, usually in the evening.

The dun This is similar to the Pale Watery, but is a little larger and has a much paler body. The male is the only upwinged fly, apart from the Pale Watery, to have yellow eyes. The male and female are similar, with pale-grey wings, pale-straw-coloured bodies, pale-olive legs becoming greyish towards the feet, and olive-grey tails. The female has olive-green eyes.

The spinner This is similar to the Pale Watery spinner, but often has a distinctive greenish tinge or stain along the leading edges of the main wings (as does the dun). A further help to identification are six to eight small cross-veins along the top leading edges of the main wings (*Drawings 14 and 15 page 34*).

Artificials No specific patterns, but a **Last Hope** (pale) or **Pale Watery Dun** should be suitable for the dun, and a **Lunn's Yellow Boy** for the spinner.

Section 5 Duns and spinners with three tails, no hindwings and very broad main wings. **Caenis** or **Broadwings** – six species.

ANGLER'S CURSE
Caenis and *Brachycercus* spp

91 Angler's Curse – Caenis Dun

92 Caenis Spinner

Habitat Lakes and rivers.
Distribution/identification This Family has six

distinct species *Brachycercus harrisella*, *Caenis horaria*, *C. robusta*, *C. rivulorum*, *C. luctuosa* and *C. macrura*. They are all so similar that only an entomologist can separate them. Often referred to as the Angler's Curse, or White Curse, some of these species are very tiny indeed. They often settle on clothing and the miracle of metamorphosis can be closely observed.

The equally tiny nymphs are moss-creepers. They live in the mud, silt or moss on the lake- or river-bed and are adept at camouflage.

Feeding trout will often start taking the emerging nymphs, change to the hatching dun, and within a short time change again to the returning spent spinners. The total adult life-span is less than 90 minutes, and consequently the fly-fisher never quite knows on which stage individual trout are feeding.

Emergence At the surface in open water. Hatches tend to be in late afternoon on lakes, but on rivers heavy hatches often occur in early morning.

The dun and spinner The duns, with their three tails, greyish to creamy-coloured bodies, and whitish main wings almost as broad as the length of their bodies, are easily identified. There is little difference between the sexes, and the only differences between duns and spinners are the transparent wings, whiter bodies and slightly longer tails of the latter. They hatch in enormous numbers and the metamorphosis from dun to spinner takes but minutes shortly after hatching.

Artificials Their small size make these difficult flies to imitate. Suggested patterns are: For the emerging nymph, a **Last Hope** (pale), fished wet; for the hatching dun, a **Last Hope**, fished dry; and for the spinner an excellent pattern is Stewart Canham's **Caenis Spinner**. As a last resort, try a large pattern such as a **Persuader**.

Section 6 These duns and spinners are either localised or uncommon. They are included as they may be important in areas where they occur, but only brief details are given. **Yellow Evening Dun**; **Purple Dun**; **Ditch Dun**; **Large Green Dun**; **Late March Brown**; **Dusky Yellowstreak**.

YELLOW EVENING DUN/SPINNER
Ephemerella notata

93 Yellow Evening Spinner (female)

94 Distinctive pattern on underbody of spinner of *E. notata*

Habitat Moderately fast rivers.
Distribution/identification This species is quite common in Wales and eastern Ireland, but uncommon elsewhere. It has not been recorded from Scotland. It has three tails and upright hindwings with costal projections and is similar to, but a little smaller than, the Yellow May Dun. The rather lethargic nymph is a moss-creeper.

Emergence In open water during late afternoon or early evening from early May until the end of June.

The dun The dun has pale-grey wings, veined yellow, and the body of the male is yellow, with the last three segments pale amber. The legs are yellowish, and the tails yellowish with brown rings. The female is similar except that the body is all-yellow.

The spinner The spinner has transparent wings with yellowish veins along the leading edges and the body is yellow-olive. The male has orange-coloured eyes, while those of the female are greenish. The underbody of the spinner has a distinctive pattern (see **94** above).

Artificials. Yellow Evening Dun (J. R. Harris); or **Lunn's Yellow Boy** to represent the spinner.

PURPLE DUN/SPINNER
Paraleptophlebia cincta

Habitat Fairly fast streams and rivers.

Distribution/identification This is one species with which I am not familiar. It is a medium-sized fly similar to, but a little larger than, the Iron Blue, which has two tails and small oval hindwings. This species has three tails and upright hindwings without costal projections. It is a dark fly.

The nymph is one of the laboured swimmers and is found in fairly fast rivers and streams. The species is reputed to have a preference for hard water. It is rather uncommon and has been recorded only from South Wales, the West Country and a few areas in the North.

Emergence In open water from May to August.

The dun The wings are dark grey and the body is dark brown, tinged purple. The legs are dark olive, tinged red, and the tails are grey. The eyes of the male are reddish-brown; those of the female, dull green.

The spinner The male has transparent wings with faint brown veining, a translucent-white body, with the last three segments purple-brown, whitish

92

legs, tinged mauve, and white tails. The female's wings are the same, but it has a brownish body with a purple tinge, pale-brown legs, and yellowish tails.

Artificials Patterns recommended for the Iron Blue should suffice.

DITCH DUN/SPINNER

Habrophlebia fusca

Habitat Ditches and slow-flowing streams.

Distribution/identification This species is of doubtful value to the fly-fisher, as it is rather uncommon and occurs only in ditches and slow-flowing sections of weedy or leaf-strewn rivers and streams. It is dark-coloured, similar to a Large Iron Blue, but with three tails. It can be easily identified by the large upright hindwings which have prominent costal projections (*Drawing 7 page 32*). The nymph is a laboured swimmer. It is not a widespread species, but has been recorded from the South of England, South Wales and the North of England.

Emergence From May to September.

The dun This has dark-grey wings and a dark-grey-olive body.

The spinner The female has a reddish-brown body.

Artificials For the dun, a **Super Grizzly** or **Imperial**; for the spinner, a **Pheasant Tail**.

LARGE GREEN DUN/SPINNER
Ecdyonurus insignis

95 Large Green Dun (female)

96 Large Green Dun (male)

Habitat Stony rivers.

Distribution/identification This large-size species with two tails and large upright hindwings with costal projections is of doubtful value to the fly-fisher as it is rather uncommon and localised in its distribution. It has been recorded only from the South-West England, South Wales, the North and a few isolated areas in Scotland.

Emergence From May to October, via stones, and most commonly in July and August.

The dun This has fawn-mottled wings with a clear patch in the centre. The body is dark olive-green. However, this particular dun is seldom available to the trout as the flat, stone-clinging nymphs tend to leave the water to emerge via stones.

97 Large Green Spinner (female)

The spinner There is little difference between male and female. Both have a smoky-black patch along the top leading edges of the main wings and olive-green bodies with diagonal brown bands. The male has exceptionally long tails. The spinners are seldom on the water in sufficient quantities to interest the trout.

Artificials No specific patterns.

LATE MARCH BROWN DUN/SPINNER
Ecdyonurus venosus

Habitat Stony rivers and streams.

Distribution/identification This large-size species has two tails, fawn-mottled main wings, and large upright hindwings with costal projections. It is similar to the March Brown, but, although it is more widely distributed, hatches are never on such a large scale. It is similar to other species in the genus, but identification is helped by the venation on the main wings (*Drawing 17 page 34*). It is found in the West Country, Wales, the North and in a few isolated areas in Scotland and Ireland.

Emergence Hatches occur throughout the summer, with a probable peak in August and September, so it is unlikely to be confused with the March Brown, which peaks in March and April.

The dun Of doubtful value as the flat, stone-clinging nymphs tend to crawl out of the water.

The spinner The female has a mahogany-red body and is often known as the Great Red Spinner. It is seldom seen on the water in great numbers, but it must make a juicy mouthful for a trout.

Artificials Patterns recommended for the **March Brown**.

DUSKY YELLOWSTREAK
Heptagenia lateralis

98 Dusky Yellowstreak Spinner (female)

Habitat Stony rivers, streams and lakes.

Distribution/identification A medium-large species with two tails and large upright hindwings with costal projections. It is not particularly common, although it is widespread over the whole of the British Isles except for South and South-East England. It has not been recorded in central Ireland.

Emergence The nymph is a stone-clinger, but is unique among upwinged flies as the dun emerges on stones beneath the surface and then swims to the surface to dry its wings before taking flight. Emergence is from May to September.

The dun There is little difference between male and female. They have dark-grey wings, dark-greyish-brown bodies, dark-brown-olive legs, and grey tails.

The spinner Both male and female have transparent wings with brown veins along the leading edges, dark-brown-olive bodies, ringed reddish, brown-olive legs, and brown tails. The last three segments of the underbody of the female is orange-brown. A positive identification is provided by a distinct yellow streak on each side of the thorax below the wing-roots – from which it takes its name.

Artificials No specific patterns, but wet flies such as **Dark Watchett** (Pritt), **Snipe and Purple** or **Iron Blue Quill** should suffice for the dun, and a **Pheasant Tail Spinner** dressed on a larger-than-normal hook for the imago.

Author's note

I have not included wet-fly patterns in the lists of artificial flies given to represent the dun and spinner of each species described for two principal reasons.

First, this book is intended for fly-fishers who are interested in identifying the natural fly and then deciding on a specific imitative pattern to match the natural. However, few, if any, wet flies have been designed to match a specific natural. Most are intended either as general patterns or, at best, to represent several species of upwinged fly. Second, the number of wet flies are legion and tend to vary from area to area, so much so that if I were to recommend a pattern for one area, I would have to list a completely different one for another area.

It is not my intention to denigrate wet flies. Some of the most popular and killing patterns that have been devised are wet flies. It is just that I feel unable to cover them adequately in a book of this nature. I merely suggest that any fly-fisher who sets out to fish a fast, brawling river on which wet flies are the order of the day, enquires locally as to the best patterns to use.

CHAPTER FIVE

The Sedge or Caddis Flies
(*Trichoptera*)

In Chapter One I gave brief details of the life history of members of this Order of insects. Here I can deal more fully with the various stages in their development that are of interest to the fly-fisher. The first is the larval stage.

The larvae

The larvae are a significant source of food for trout in both streams and stillwater, and any food that is important to the trout must also be important to the fly-fisher, provided that it can be copied reasonably accurately in fur and feather and fished in such a manner that the trout will accept it for the type of food on which it is feeding. It is possible to imitate most forms of trout food fairly successfully, but these larvae do pose several problems.

First, the Order *Trichoptera* includes nearly 200 different species, with an enormous diversity of form and habit. Second, most of the larvae are found either on or close to the bed of the river or lake; and third, they do not swim but crawl, and even then exceedingly slowly.

It is hardly surprising that few patterns have

A typical sedge larva with its case (4×)

been devised to represent these strange creatures. But it is surprising that any of them do take trout, as (apart from fishing an almost static larva pattern to simulate the natural on the bottom, which is seldom successful) they are normally fished off the bottom and even in mid-water. However, fished in this manner, some of these patterns have proved very successful, particularly on lakes and reservoirs.

The larvae of the *Trichoptera* are known by a variety of common names – caddis grubs, caddis worms, stick worms – and they are found in a wide range of aquatic habitats – under or on submerged stones, among or on water-weeds, or just lying on the silt, gravel or mud of the bottom. Of the 193 British species, 148 make cases out of extraneous materials such as vegetable debris, small stones, pieces of gravel, cut sections of leaf, small sticks and even discarded shells. The remaining species are free-swimming, and most of them construct either bag-like nets, usually communicating with tube-like shelters, or tubes of silk-like material which are used as fixed and permanent homes. Four species are entirely free-living.

The case-making larvae use an astonishing variety of materials, but those that live in running water construct their cases from heavy materials that give maximum stability in fast currents. Most larvae complete their life-cycle within one year, but a few species seem to have two or more broods within the year and it is suspected some may have even a two-year cycle. Some species are herbivorous, feeding on vegetable matter; others are carnivorous, or omnivorous to varying degrees.

The importance of caddis larvae has been known to fishermen for more than 300 years, and in the formative years of angling, the caddis grub was a favourite bait with coarse fishermen. It is only within the last two decades or so that fly-dressers have evolved patterns to represent these larvae and, so far as I am aware, these have been perfected only for use in stillwater.

Artificial larvae

One of the earliest artificials was one called the **Stick Fly**, and it remains an excellent pattern. A similar, but more sophisticated pattern is Bob Carnill's **Cased Caddis**, which is my current favourite. Other patterns are Richard Walker's **Sand Caddis** and the **Caddis Larva**, devised by Raleigh Boaze to represent the free-swimming species. Two good general patterns are the **Woolly Worm** and Brian Clarke's **Ombudsman**. All these patterns should be fished very slowly on a long leader close to the bottom, although, strange to relate, the first two have also proved effective as point-flies in a team of three Sedge patterns fished just below the surface from a boat drifting down-wind.

COMMON SPECIES OF CADDIS LARVAE

99 Larva of *R. dorsalis*

101 Larva of *P. grandis*

100 Larvae of
S. personatum and
latipennis
(large case)

102 Larvae of
L. hirtum, L. lunatus
and *G. pellucidus*
(leaf case)

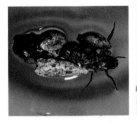

103 Larva of *G. pilosa*   **104** Larva of *H. radiatus*

The Caddis or Sedge Pupae

Sedge pupae are far more important to the fly-fisher than are the larvae, particularly in still-water. The pupal stage is comparatively short, lasting usually between 12 and 16 days. When the time comes for it to pupate, a case-making larva seals the ends of its larval case with pieces of moss, tufts of algae, cut pieces of weed, or even small stones or gravel, and sometimes with a web of its own chitinous substance. Most free-swimming species form cocoons made from various substances, including small stones, which are then attached to the undersides of large stones or boulders on the river-bed.

Pupation

Various changes take place during pupation until, in the final stages, the pupa assumes the main characteristics of the adult. The wings are fully formed, but folded within the case; the body is

A typical Sedge pupa (4×)

complete and coloured; and the antennae are fully developed and folded or, in those species with long antennae, wound spirally around the body. The head of the pupa has a pair of powerful mandibles which it uses to cut its way out of the case or cocoon. The legs are also formed and are free, although the pupal integument closely follows their shape. The median legs are entirely free and, provided with a denser fringe of hairs than are the other legs, are used rather like paddles to enable the pupa to swim either to the surface or towards the shore.

Some species hatch into the adult at the surface in open water, while others migrate to the shore, where they seek out an object projecting above the surface and there complete their metamorphosis. The pupal skin loosely enveloping the formed imago expands from internal pressure, possibly air or gas, until it splits along the top of the head and the fully adult fly emerges.

Artificial pupae

These pupae are much easier to imitate with fur and feather than are the larvae. Furthermore, it is much simpler to imitate their swimming action as they travel to the surface or towards the shore. Despite the multiplicity of families and species, they vary little in appearance apart from size and colour, so the fly-dresser has only to vary these two factors once a satisfactory tying has been achieved. For the same reason, there is little point in trying to identify individual species. In any case, to do so is extremely difficult and would tax the skills even of a trained entomologist. Added to this, while empty pupal skins are often seen drifting on the surface, it is seldom possible to capture pupae on their way to the surface.

So far as I am aware, the first artificial devised specifically to imitate a sedge pupa was devised in the mid-1920s by the renowned Dr Howard Bell, of Blagdon fame. He called his pattern the **Amber Nymph**, and it takes its quota of trout to this day. A famous old Irish pattern, called the **Green Peter**, which can be fished wet or dry according to the position of the hen hackle, is undoubtedly much older, although it could be argued that it was never intended to represent the sedge pupa. Nevertheless, it is an excellent pattern.

The second custom-devised pupa pattern was probably **Sharp's Favourite**, introduced in the early '60s. It was followed in the mid-'60s by my own range of **Sedge Pupa** patterns dressed in different colours and sizes to represent the many different species. These were followed in the early '70s by Dick Walker's **Longhorn Pupa** series and more recently by his **Shorthorn** patterns to represent the smaller pupae. These three different series are undoubtedly the most popular patterns in current use. The last two are probably more useful when the trout are taking the emerging or hatching pupa. Two other patterns tied specifically to represent the hatching stage are the **Hatching Sedge Pupa** (John Roberts) and another **Hatching Sedge Pupa** (Brian Clarke and myself). The last is particularly useful in running water.

STAGES IN SEDGE PUPA DEVELOPMENT

105 Typical sedge pupa swimming to surface

106 Pupa on surface in first stage of transposition into adult

107 Pupa in final stage, with case inflated before splitting at thorax

108 A pupa's hair-fringed median legs used for swimming

109 Longhorn sedge pupa emerging from case

110 A later stage, with wings and head of the pupa out of its case

The Adult Caddis or Sedge-fly

The adults of the Order *Trichoptera* vary greatly in size, the largest British species having a body-length of more than an inch, and some of the smaller species being less than 5 mm. They are similar to moths. In fact, it is extremely difficult to tell the difference in some of the smaller species

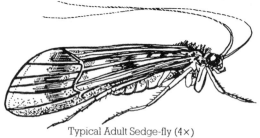

Typical Adult Sedge-fly (4×)

without examining them through a low-power glass. However, there is one infallible method of establishing whether a specimen is a moth or a sedge: the wings of a sedge-fly are covered with tiny hairs, while those of a moth are covered with tiny scales.

The adult sedge-fly has four wings, the forewings being slightly longer than the anterior wings and, when the fly is at rest, these completely cover the body rather like a roof in an inverted V-shape. The abdomen is composed of nine segments and is tailless. A distinct thorax is composed of three segments, while a pair of long antennae are in some species more than twice the body length. The eyes are large and compound. Protruding from the mouth are two pairs of palps, called the maxillary and labial respectively. The middle joints of the six legs often have quite long, slender spurs, and their number can help an entomologist establish the genus.

Despite the fact that nearly 200 British species are known, there is no great variation in the adults apart from size. The basic colour of the wings varies from black through brown to grey or pale fawn. The wings of some species are heavily veined, while those of others may be distinctly mottled. The body colours range from yellow through green or brown to dark grey.

From the fly-fisher's point of view, sedge-flies may be divided into two groups: species that hatch during the day, and those that hatch at night. They can be sub-divided into those that hatch in open water and those that hatch either on shore or via emergent vegetation, posts, stones or any other objects extending above the water surface. Many that hatch during the day tend to be the smaller, darker species. Fortunately, many of the larger species that hatch at night do so in late evening, as dusk approaches, so coming within the scope of the fly-fisher.

Species that hatch in open water are of particular value as they make tempting targets for hungry trout. A few of the larger species seem to have a problem in drying their wings and remain on the surface for a considerable time, causing quite a disturbance. Some species that migrate shorewards to hatch do so by swimming on the surface, leaving a noticeable V-shaped wake, and these, too, attract the attention of the trout. Species that hatch out of the water are of little interest to the fly-fisher except when the females return to lay their eggs. Most sedge-flies mate on the wing, sinking slowly to the ground where copulation is usually completed.

Precise identification of the sedge flies is of little value, as trout rarely become preoccupied with one particular species as they do with upwinged flies. The reason is probably the physical differences between the two Orders. The upwinged flies have large upright wings which are clearly visible to a trout through its window, and their bodies are not shielded by their wings, so that their colours clearly stand out. Conversely, the wings of a sedge-fly at rest are held low over its body and are all but invisible to a trout until they pass over the edge of its window. Furthermore, the wings shield the fly's body from the trout, so that it can see only the lower part of the abdomen. So usually it is enough for the fly-dresser simply to achieve the right size and body colour in his artificial, although it may also be important to ensure that the colour or pattern of the winging material matches the natural.

The Adult Sedge-flies

The following list includes most of the common and abundant species of sedge-fly of interest to the fly-fisher. It may seem restricted in view of the fact that nearly 200 British species are known, but of these many are scarce, locally distributed, or too small to be of practical interest to the fly-fisher.

The list is also rather different from lists that appeared in my first two books. This is due partly to the fact that it incorporates both running and

111 A sedge with wings fully extended

112 A pair of mating sedges: *Sericostoma personatum*

stillwater species and partly to much additional information I have either researched or acquired over the years. I have made several changes and have dropped some species from my original list. One is the Small Silver Sedge, as I have now concluded that it is too localised in its distribution to warrant inclusion. On the other hand, I have added several new species, including three that are extremely common and abundant. For want of a better name, I have grouped these under the heading of "Yellow-spotted Sedge"

Following the list are brief details of all the species named, in order of size, including information on habitat and times of emergence. I hope this information will be of value to those fly-fishers who wish, for their own satisfaction, to establish which of these more common species appear on their particular waters.

THE FISHERMAN'S SEDGE-FLIES (*Trichoptera*)

Angler's name	Approximate anterior wing-length
Great Red Sedge or Murragh	20–27 mm
Caperer	20–23 mm
Large Cinnamon Sedge	18–19 mm
Mottled Sedge	17 mm
Silver Sedge or Grey Sedge	13–18 mm
Brown Sedge	12–16 mm
Cinnamon Sedge	14–15 mm
Welshman's Button	12–15 mm
Longhorns	11–13 mm
Grey Flag	11–12 mm
Marbled Sedge	11–12 mm
Medium Sedge	10–12 mm
Sandfly	Variable
Grannom	9–11 mm
Black Sedge	8–10 mm
Brown Silverhorns	8–10 mm
Black Silverhorns	8–9 mm
Grouse-wing or Grouse and Green	8–9 mm
Small Red Sedge	8 mm
Yellow-spotted sedge	6–8 mm
Small Yellow Sedge	5–6 mm

Entomologist's name

Phrygania grandis/P. striata
Halesus radiatus/H. digitatus
Potamophylax latipennis
Glyphotalius pellucidus
Odontocerum albicorne
Anabolia nervosa or *Hydropsyche augustpennis*
Limnephilus lunatus/L. marmoratus
Seriscostoma personatum
Oecetis ochracea/O. lacustris
Hydropsyche instabilis/H. pellucidula
Hydropsyche contubernalis
Goera pilosa
Rhyacophila dorsalis
Brachycentrus subnubilus
Silo nigricornis or *S. pallipes*
Athripsodes cinereus, A annulicornis or
A. albifrons
Mystacides azurea, Athripsodes atterimus or
A. nigronervosus
Mystacides longicornis

Tinodes waeneri
Cyrnus trimaculatus, Holocentropus picicornis
or *Polycentropus flavomaculatus*
Psychomyia pusilla

GREAT RED SEDGE
Phrygania grandis or *P. striata*

This is our largest British common species and has a wing-span of nearly 2 inches (50 mm).

Body Greyish.

Wings Vary between 20-27 mm. Brownish-red. Female has blackish bar running along centre of anterior wing. In *P. striata* this bar is broken in the centre.

Antennae Stout and as long as or slightly shorter than wings.

Habitat Lakes ponds and slow rivers.

Flight May to July.

Distribution Widespread.

Emergence In open water during late afternoon and early evening.

113 Great Red Sedge   **114** Caperer

CAPERER
Halesus radiatus or *H. digitatus*

This is almost as large as the Great Red Sedge and is common on the chalk-streams of southern England.

Body Orange-brown to greenish-brown.

Wings Vary between 20-23 mm. Brown to yellowish-brown with black striate mark towards apex.

Antennae Stout and as long as or slightly shorter than wings.

Habitat Rivers.

Flight Late August to October.

Distribution Widespread.

Emergence In open water during late afternoon or evening.

LARGE CINNAMON SEDGE
Potamophylax latipennis

One of our most common sedge-flies. It is a little smaller than, but similar to, the Caperer, but has a small pale patch in centre of its wings.
Body Greyish-green.
Wings 18-19 mm brownish-yellow with distinct pale spot in centre.
Antennae Fairly stout and a little shorter than the wings.
Habitat Mainly rivers, but some lakes.
Flight Late June to September
Distribution Widespread and abundant.
Emergence In open water during evening.

115 Large Cinnamon Sedge   **116** Mottled Sedge

MOTTLED SEDGE
Glyphotalius pellucidus

More likely to be found in tree-lined ponds and lakes than in large bodies of water. It is a most distinctive-looking species.
Body Dull green.
Wings About 17 mm. The dark-brown blotches on a pale background are more prominent on the male. It cannot be mistaken for any other species, due to the excised apices of the anterior wings.
Antennae Shorter than the wings and fairly stout.
Habitat Ponds and lakes only.
Flight May to October.
Distribution Widespread.
Emergence Late afternoon and evening.

GREY OR SILVER SEDGE
Odontocerum albicorne

This is a fairly large species with reddish-brown eyes and is found only in fairly fast-flowing water.

Body Dark-greyish.

Wings Silvery to dark-grey, often with black striate marking in centre of the anterior wings which are 13-18 mm long.

Antennae Long and toothed. Each segment has a small spur-like tooth.

Habitat Fairly fast-running water with a preference for stony bottom.

Flight June to October.

Distribution Widespread.

Emergence During day and early evening in open water.

117 Grey or Silver Sedge   **118** Brown Sedge

BROWN SEDGE
Anabolia nervosa

A medium-sized species, but one which varies considerably. Often swarms over the water in great clouds in early evening.

Body Dark brown.

Wings 12-15 mm. Brown with large pale spot in centre.

Antennae Stout and about the same length as the wings.

Habitat Common in both rivers and lakes.

Flight June and July, and September/October.

Distribution Widespread and abundant.

Emergence During early evening via emergent vegetation.

A similar species, *Hydropsyche augustpennis*, can be distinguished by a slightly elevated and blackened ridge which winds spirally round the antennae.

CINNAMON SEDGE
Limnephilus lunatus

This is one of the earliest of the more common species and, with its distinctive mottled wings, one of the easier sedges to recognise.

Body Varies from orange-brown to green.

Wings 14-15 mm. Rather narrow. Rich yellow to a cinnamon-brown with irregular brownish patches and a distinctive pale lunate patch at apex of wings.

Antennae About the same length as the wings.

Habitat Rivers, ponds and lakes.

Flight Late May to November.

Distribution Widespread and abundant.

Emergence During day and early evening close to emergent vegetation.

L. marmoratus is a similar species, but without the lunar patch on the wings.

 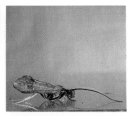

119 Cinnamon Sedge   **120** Welshman's Button

WELSHMAN'S BUTTON
Seriscostoma personatum

Few fly-fishers can have failed to have heard of this well-known sedge-fly. It was named by the great F. M. Halford in the late 1800s.

Body Dark grey, sometimes tinged greenish.

Wings Variable between 12-15 mm. Dark or golden-chestnut-brown and rather hairy.

Antennae As long as wings; moderately stout.
Habitat Fast rivers, and streams and lakes where rivers run in.
Flight June to August.
Distribution Fairly widespread.
Emergence During day and early evening.

LONGHORN SEDGE
Oecetis ochracea

This is a species which I took the liberty of naming in the late '60s as I found it common on many of the big reservoirs.
Body Greyish-green.
Wings Very narrow, 11-13 mm long. Pale-greyish-yellow to fawn.
Antennae Long and slender and up to three times the length of the wings.
Habitat Lakes, ponds and reservoirs.
Flight June to September.
Distribution Fairly widespread.
Emergence During afternoon and early evening.

O. lacustris is similar but slightly smaller, with darker-brownish wings.

121 Longhorn Sedge   **122** Grey Flag Sedge

GREY FLAG
Hydropsyche instabilis

While hatches of this species tend to be sparse, it is a useful sedge for the fly-fisher as it is one of the day-flying species.
Body Greyish-brown.

Wings 11-12 mm. Dark grey with well-defined dark markings.

Antennae About the same length as the wings with a blackened ridge winding spirally around the segments.

Habitat Fairly swift rivers.

Flight June to August.

Distribution Widespread and abundant.

Emergence During the day and early evening.

A similar species, *H. pellucidula*, is found in slower-flowing water and in lakes.

MARBLED SEDGE
Hydropsyche contubernalis

A colourful-looking sedge (**123**) with strongly-patterned wings which give it a distinctive marbled appearance – hence the common name which I decided to bestow upon it.

Body Dark-greenish.

Wings 11-12 mm. Brownish-green with dark patches.

Antennae Fairly stout and about the same length as the body.

Habitat The larvae are free-swimmers and are found usually in running water.

Flight June to August.

Distribution Widespread and fairly abundant, particularly on many Scottish and Welsh rivers.

Emergence Afternoon and early evening on sunny days. Often seen flying in vicinity of trees and bushes.

123 Marbled Sedge   **124** Cinnamon Sedge – a trout's-eye view

MEDIUM SEDGE
Goera pilosa

As the common name implies, this is a medium-sized species. It is a useful sedge for the fly-fisher as it is one of the day-flying species.
Body Yellowish-grey.
Wings 10-12 mm long and quite broad and hairy. Dark-greyish-yellow to brownish-yellow, with a small pale patch in centre.
Antennae Short and stout.
Habitat Rivers and lakes.
Flight May to August.
Distribution Widespread and abundant.
Emergence During the day and early evening.

125 A longhorn sedge on surface, showing extraordinary length of antennae

126 Pupal case of a sandfly sedge attached to large stone

SANDFLY
Rhyacophila dorsalis

The common name for this species was first established in Ronald's *Fly Fishers' Entomology*. He had a high regard for it.
Body Greenish.
Wings Variable, 9-15 mm. Rather narrow and sandy-brown.
Antennae Slender and a little shorter than the wings.
Habitat Streams and rivers.
Flight April to October.
Distribution Widespread and abundant.
Emergence Late afternoon and evening.

GRANNOM
Brachycentrus subnubilus

This species has a short season and is one of the earliest sedge-flies to appear. It hatches during the day in countless thousands.

Body Fawn to green.

Wings 9-11 mm long and greyish-yellow with dark-brown blotches.

Antennae Length of wings and quite stout.

Habitat Rivers and streams.

Flight Late March and April, but later in the far North of England.

Distribution Widespread but localised.

Emergence Noon onwards in open water.

127 Medium Sedge

128 Sandfly

BLACK SEDGE
Silo nigricornis

A day-hatching species which is rather triangular in appearance.

Body Greyish-black.

Wings 8-10 mm long. Wide, hairy and black in males; females, dark-brown.

Habitat Running water.

Flight May to early July.

Distribution Widespread and abundant.

Emergence During afternoon and early evening.

129 Grannom

130 Black Sedge

A similar species, *S. pallipes*, is more likely to be found on smaller streams.

BROWN SILVERHORNS
Athripsodes cinereus

These medium to small-sized sedges are among our most common species and can be seen flying low over the water in huge swarms from late afternoon onwards.

Body Brownish-green.

Wings 8-10 mm long. Narrow and brown.

Antennae Long and slender. Twice the length of wings and strongly ringed white.

Habitat Rivers and lakes.

Flight June to August

Distribution Widespread and abundant.

Emergence Afternoon and early evening.

Two similar species are *A. annulicornis*, which has the apices of the wings fringed white, and *A. albifrons*, which has snowy-white markings or patches.

131 Brown Silverhorns   **132** Black Silverhorns

BLACK SILVERHORNS
Mystacides azurea

Another common species, but not so common in the South of England as the Brown Silverhorns. This genus has large red eyes.

Body Dark-grey to black.

Wings 8-9 mm long. Narrow and black, with a steel-blue sheen.

Antennae Long and slim. More than twice length of wings and faintly ringed white.

Habitat Rivers and lakes.

Flight June to August.

Distribution Widespread and abundant.
Emergence Afternoon and early evening.

There are two other similar species, but neither has bright red eyes. *A. atterimus* has a dull yellow spot at the arculus (top end), and *A. nigronervosus* is a little larger and has black antennae that are not ringed.

GROUSE-WING
Mystacides longicornis

This species is very common and is easily identified as the long, slim wings are strongly marked like a grouse feather – hence its common name.
Body Grey-brown.
Wings 8-9 mm long. Narrow with three distinct dark transverse bands.
Antennae More than twice the length of the body. Slim and white with brown ringing.
Habitat Lakes and ponds.
Flight June to September.
Distribution Widespread and abundant.
Emergence Afternoon and early evening.

133 Grouse-wing   **134** Small Red Sedge

SMALL RED SEDGE
Tinodes waeneri

This is the Little Red Sedge so beloved of that great fly-fisher of the chalk-streams, G. E. M. Skues.
Body Dark-greyish-brown.
Wings About 8 mm. Rather narrow and hairy. Golden to red-brown.
Antennae Stout and shorter than wings.

Habitat Ponds, lakes and slower sections of rivers.
Flight May to October.
Distribution Widespread and abundant.
Emergence Late afternoon and evening.

YELLOW-SPOTTED SEDGE
Cyrnus trimaculatus

135 Yellow-spotted Sedge

I have added this sedge-fly to the list under this suggested name as it is an extremely common species.
Body Dark reddish-brown.
Wings 6-8 mm. Rather narrow and hairy. Brown with golden-yellow spots.
Antennae Brown, stout, and about the same length as the wings.
Habitat Lakes, ponds and slow-flowing rivers.
Flight July to September.
Distribution Widespread and abundant.
Emergence Late afternoon or in evening.

Two other equally abundant and similar species are *Holocentropus picicornis*, which is a little larger, with a wing-length of 7-9 mm, and *Polycentropus flavomaculatus*, which is even larger, with wings of 9-12 mm.

SMALL YELLOW SEDGE
Psychomyia pusilla

This is the smallest and commonest sedge-fly of any practical value to the fly-fisher.

Body Creamy to brownish-yellow.
Wings 5-6 mm long. Brownish to golden-yellow
Antennae Pale yellow, stout, shorter than wings, and ringed brown.
Habitat Rivers and streams.
Flight Late May to September.
Distribution Widespread and abundant.
Emergence Early to late evening

This species can be identified by a strong spur-shaped excision halfway along the leading edge of the anterior wings.

136 Small Yellow Sedge

Artificial Sedge-flies

As I have explained, there is little need for strictly imitative patterns to represent most sedge-flies, as trout feeding on them are not very discriminating. However, it is important to present a pattern of the right size and general colouration to match the most common species seen to be hatching.

Artificial patterns of sedge-fly are legion, and to list all of them would provide an unnecessarily wide choice. A few patterns have been developed to represent specific naturals, but even these are not strictly imitative patterns. They are:

Green Peter, which is meant to represent one of the species of the Great Red Sedge.

Caperer (Lunn), intended to copy the natural sedge of the same name, and which, although it is not a very good copy, seems effective.

Grannom (Pat Russell), an excellent pattern which represents the natural of the same name.

Brown Sedge (Terry Thomas), tied to represent the natural Brown Sedge.

Black Silverhorns (Alfred Ronalds), a good copy of the naturals of the same name.

Cinnamon Sedge, of which several patterns represent the naturals of the same name.

Little Brown Sedge (Courtney Williams), an excellent pattern to represent the Brown Sedge when it is on the water.

Mottled Sedge (Jocelyn Lane), a particularly good pattern when the natural is hatching.

Silver Sedge, representing any of the light-coloured sedges.

Little Red Sedge (Skues), perfected to represent the Small Red Sedge and one of the best all-round patterns.

There are many excellent general patterns, a few of which are:

Walker's Sedge, a popular pattern devised by the late and great Richard Walker.

G&H Sedge, my own pattern, dressed by the late Cliff Henry and an excellent floating pattern for use on large lakes or large, fast rivers and, under the name **Goddard Caddis**, now one of the most popular sedge patterns in the United States.

Poly-caddis, a pattern I have recently devised and which has proved exceptionally killing and is easy to tie. It is dressed with either a normal hackle or a fully-palmered hackle and in two colours and different sizes.

It is essential to have some wet sedge patterns for big lakes and reservoirs, but while there are many from which to choose, the best are without doubt **Wickham's Fancy**, or **Invicta**, or, a more recent pattern, the **Shredge** (Tony Knight). An excellent general stillwater pattern is the **Red Palmer** (which should always be fished well oiled on the top dropper) and so is the **Terry's Terror**. Finally, on large stillwaters, a **Muddler Minnow** fished fast at the surface in a big wave is always worth a try in late summer.

CHAPTER SIX

The Stoneflies
(*Plecoptera*)
The Hard-winged Flies

The Stoneflies, or hard-winged flies, as they are commonly called, form one of the most primitive groups of winged insects. They are also one of the smaller Orders, with not many more than 30 British species, of which only about 11 are of interest to the fly-fisher, the rest being either rare or very local in their distribution. Despite this, stoneflies are of considerable importance to river fly-fishers, particularly in Wales and many parts of northern Britain. Elsewhere, their value is doubtful.

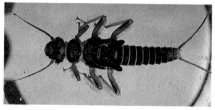

137 Large Stonefly Nymph (*P. microcephala*)

138 Large Stonefly Nymph (*P. bipunctata*)

As their name implies, their preferred habitat is in fast or fairly fast rivers with stony or rocky bottoms. However, a few species have adapted to living in slower water, and even in silty or weedy rivers, so it is not surprising that some of those species of interest to the fly-fisher are also to be found in stillwaters, mainly on stony lake shores.

They vary greatly in size. Some of the larger species have a wing-span of nearly 2 inches, while the Needle fly (**148**), the smallest species in the Order, has a wing-span of barely ¾ inch. Their anatomical structure is similar to that of sedge-flies, but there the comparison ends as they are much more robust. The legs are stouter and the wings are hard and shiny and lie flat along the top of the body. They also have two antennae, but these are much shorter than in the sedges, usually less than half the length of the body. In addition, they have two tails (unlike the sedge-flies, which have none), although these are sometimes so short that they are reduced to mere stumps and are difficult to distinguish.

139 Small Stonefly Nymph (*Isoperla grammatica*)   **140** Large Stonefly (adult female) (*P. microcephala*)

All stoneflies have four wings, but in some of the smaller species they tend to be moulded round the body when the flies are at rest, rather than lying on top as in most of the larger species. The males of some of the larger species are incapable of flight, as the wings are virtually non-existent. In Scotland, the Border counties and throughout Yorkshire and Lancashire, the large adult Stoneflies are sometimes known as Mayflies.

The Stonefly Nymph, or Creeper as it is often called (**137**, **138**, **139**), is of little value to the fly-fisher as it is all but impossible to imitate the natural, which spends its life crawling on the bed of the river or lake. But the nymph, where it occurs, is certainly an important source of food for the trout, as is the female adult returning to the water to oviposit. It is at this time in its life-cycle that the stonefly is important to the fly-fisher. On many North Country rivers, where hatches are large and regular, the trout will take the egg-laying females ravenously as they dip down on to the water, and the spent fly drifting on the surface.

LARGE STONEFLY
Perla bipunctata

141 Large Stonefly   **142** Yellow Sally
(*P microcephala*)

This and the following species are the largest of the British stoneflies, having a wing-span some-times exceeding 2 inches. The wings are mottled brown and the body is grey to greyish-yellow. The male varies in length from 16-23 mm, the female from 18-24 mm. Found in rivers and streams with unstable stony sub-strata, the species is common and abundant except in the Midlands, South-East England and most of Ireland. It is on the wing from mid-April to June.

LARGE STONEFLY
Dinocras cephalotes

This is similar to, and the same size as, the preceding species, but can be quickly identified from the top of the first segment of the thorax, which is black. In *P. bipunctata* this segment has black markings on a pale-yellow ground. The species prefers rivers with stable rocky or stony sub-strata. Fairly common and fairly abundant, it is found in roughly the same areas as *P. bipunctata.* The adults hatch during May and June.

LARGE STONEFLY
Perlodes microcephala

A little smaller than the two preceding species, this species also has brown-mottled wings, but the body is creamy-yellow and the legs are also tinged with yellow. The length of the male (**141**) varies from 13-18 mm, the female (**140**) from 16-23 mm. A common species, it is found in stony rivers and streams up to about 1,200 ft and on the shores of stony lakes. It is also found in the same areas as the previous two, but ranges further south and is seen occasionally on the chalk-streams. Adults are on the wing from March to May, and sometimes until July.

143 February Red

144 Willow Fly

MEDIUM STONEFLY
Diura bicaudata

This species is less common and less widespread than most others, and it is found only at altitudes above 1,000 ft. The wings are mottled brown and the body is greyish-yellow (**149**). The length of the male varies from 10-13 mm, the female from 12-14

126

mm. The species is likely to be encountered on stony streams and on the shores of stony lakes. It is rather local in distribution, but common and abundant where it does occur, mainly in Scotland, West Wales, the Lake District and parts of Ireland. The adults appear from April to June.

YELLOW SALLY
Isoperla grammatica

This medium-sized species is one of the easiest to recognise because of its all-yellow colouration (**142**). The male is 8-11 mm, the female 9-13mm. Found in stony rivers and streams, and on the shores of stony lakes, the species is common and abundant and found all over the British Isles apart from East Anglia and parts of the Midlands. The adults are on the wing from April to August.

FEBRUARY RED
Taeniopteryx nebulosa

This species is quite common in some areas, but does tend to be rather localised. It is medium to small. The wings are reddish-brown and mottled, sometimes with two distinctive dark bands (**143**). The body is brownish, with the last three segments reddish-brown. The male is 7-9 mm, the female 9-11 mm. This is probably the only Stonefly that dislikes a stony environment, seeming to prefer rivers with emergent vegetation. It is found mainly in the North of England and in parts of Wales, the West Country and Scotland. An early-season species, adults are likely to be seen on the wing from February to April.

Brachyptera risi, a similar species, has the same common name and is in fact more common and widespread. It also has a longer season, extending from March to July. It is about the same size, but may be found also in stony rivers.

WILLOW FLY
Leuctra geniculata

This is another small to medium-sized species, but is one of the most common of all Stoneflies. Like the Needle Fly, this species (**144**) appears much slimmer than other Stoneflies, as the brown, dark-veined wings tend to mould around the greyish-brown body. The male is 7-9 mm, while the female is 8-11 mm. The species can be found in large streams and rivers with stony sub-strata and is most in evidence from August to October. It is common and abundant in the South, South West, Wales and the North.

145 Early Brown

146 Small Brown

147 Small Yellow Sally

148 Needle Fly

EARLY BROWN
Protonemura meyeri

This small and common species can be seen early in the season. The wings are greyish-brown, and a useful point of identification is a transverse pale bar across the top of the head (**145**). The male varies from 5-8 mm, the female from 7-9 mm. It is a common and abundant species and is usually found in swift-flowing rivers, especially where aquatic mosses occur, and often up to quite high altitudes. It occurs throughout the British Isles except for East Anglia and parts of Ireland. The peak flight period is from March to May.

SMALL BROWN
Nemoura cinerea

The Small Brown is similar to the Early Brown, but has a slimmer appearance and wings are darker-brown (**146**). The male is 6-7 mm long, the female 6-9 mm. The species is found in still or slow-flowing water with much emergent vegetation and in sluggish, stony streams. It is common and abundant, occurring throughout the British Isles. Adults are on the wing from March to July, and sometimes to September.

There are several closely-related species, some of which prefer faster-flowing water. As far as the fly-fisher is concerned, they can all be termed Small Browns. They are *Nemurella picteti*, *Nemoura avicularis*, *N. cambrica* and a slightly smaller species often found in larger streams and rivers, *Amphinemura sulcicollis*.

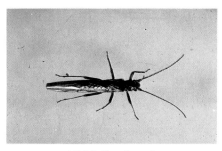

149 Medium Stonefly

150 Medium Stonefly Nymphs or Creepers

SMALL YELLOW SALLY
Chloroperla torrentium

One of the smallest of all Stoneflies, this species is easily identified as, apart from the much larger Yellow Sally, it is the only other yellow-coloured fly in its Order (**147**). The male varies from 5-7 mm in length, the female from 6-8 mm. The species is found in all types of water with stony sub-strata and occurs throughout the British Isles apart from East Anglia and the lower Midlands. Neither does it occur in central Ireland. Adults may be seen on the wing from April to June and occasionally as late as August. It is a common and abundant species and is a useful fly-fisher's fly, particularly on rivers in Wales and the West Country.

NEEDLE FLY
Leuctra fusca

When at rest, this species is so slim that it really does appear needle-like, hence its common name. Like the Willow Fly, it has wings that seem to mould around the body (**148**). Both wings and body are dark-brown. The male varies from 6-8 mm, the female from 7-9 mm. The species occurs in all types of water with stony sub-strata and its range is similar to that of the preceding species. The peak flight period is from August to October.

Several other species in the genus may be classified under the same common name, as only a trained entomologist can separate them. However, these are all early-season species and are to be seen on the wing from February to July. They are *Leuctra hippopus*, *L. inermis* and *L. nigra*. The last two species are a little smaller. All three species are confined to running water.

The artificials

There is little need for specific imitations of the Stoneflies. Apart from the two all-yellow species, the Yellow Sally and the Small Yellow Sally, most of the naturals have a similar colouration: a greyish to yellow-brown body and brown or mottled-brown wings. So, as with the Sedge-flies, the most desirable features of an artificial are that it should float well and be of the correct size to match the hatching natural.

Dame Juliana Berners gave a Stonefly dressing in her famous *Treatise* as long ago as the fifteenth century, and, subsequently, equally famous anglers, such as Markham, Cotton and Ronalds, also produced dressings. In this century alone literally scores of dressings have been devised, but with just a few exceptions, none has proved consistently successful. My own recommendation is for a small selection of general patterns in a range of sizes: **Grey Duster**; **Blue Upright** (Austin); **John Storey**; **Partridge and Orange**; and **Dark Spanish Needle** (Pritt); with Taff Price's **Yellow Sally** to represent the two yellow species.

More specific patterns still widely used in the North Country are: **Stonefly** (Roger Woolley); **Willow Fly** (Alfred Ronalds); and **Medium Stonefly** (T. Price). It is all but impossible to imitate successfully the nymphs, or creepers as they are often called, but the natural mounted on a hook can be a deadly method of taking trout on waters where it is allowed.

CHAPTER SEVEN

The Flat-winged Flies
(*Diptera*)
Heather, Hawthorn, Drone and Crane Flies, Gnats and Smuts

This is by far the largest and most diverse Order of flies, containing many thousands of different species. Some are so small that they are difficult to see with the naked eye, while others – the Crane-flies for instance – are extremely large, with a wing-span of nearly 2 inches. Despite this, the *Diptera* include relatively few Families of interest to the fly-fisher.

However some of them are extremely important. The Midges, or *Chironomids*, for example, include

151 Typical Flat-winged fly: the Oak Fly

152 Cowdung Fly (*Cordiluridae spp*)

many species that together form a staple diet for trout in both running and stillwater. In fact, in many large lakes and reservoirs, the trout would find it difficult to survive without flies of this Family.

These many species commonly referred to as true flies, and, as the entomological name *Diptera* implies, they have only two wings. These are usually transparent, often overlap, and lie flat along the top of the body, hence the fly-fisher's name for them – the Flat-winged Flies.

The Order contains many Families that are household names – Mosquitoes, Crane-flies (Daddy-long-legs), Horse-flies, Dung-flies, Gnats, Smuts, Midges and, of course, the common House-flies. Only a few Families have aquatic origins. Most are terrestrial and are of interest to the trout and to the fly-fisher only when they are blown on to the water. I shall not detail the various life-cycles of the flies in this Order (other than a few of the aquatic species), as they are of no practical value to the fly-fisher.

153 Hawthorn Fly **154** Heather Fly

HAWTHORN FLY
Bibio marci

In old angling literature this species (**153**) was referred to as St Mark's Fly, probably because it usually appears in numbers towards the end of April, and St Mark's day is on April 25. Adults can be seen on the wing for about three weeks, often in quite large swarms and usually in the vicinity of trees or bushes. They are similar in size to the common Bluebottle (10-12 mm), but slimmer. They are jet-black and hairy. The male has transparent wings with black leading edges, while those of the female are greyish. They can be quickly recognised on the wing by their long, trailing rear legs.

Although it is a terrestrial species, the Hawthorn Fly is often found adjacent to water and is frequently blown on to the surface, where it is much appreciated by the trout. The many artificials all go under the name **Hawthorn Fly**. There is also the **USD Hawthorn**.

HEATHER FLY
Bibio pomonae

This terrestrial species (**154**) is similar to the Hawthorn and also has long, trailing rear-legs. However, it can easily be identified as the tops of all its leg joints are bright red, hence the fly's common Scottish name – Bloody Doctor. It is often found in the vicinity of heather, and is common in many parts of Wales, Scotland and the North, although I have frequently seen swarms of them on the Test in the South of England. The main flight period is from late July to September, when the fly forms an important part of the trout's diet on lochs and reservoirs in heather-clad country. A standard **Hawthorn** with a small red hackle added is a good artificial.

155 Black Gnat   **156** Drone Fly

BLACK GNAT
Bibio johannis

While *Bibio johannis* is probably the most common species, many others are so similar that only an entomologist can segregate them. *Bibio johannis* and *B. reticulatus* are to be seen in spring, while *B. clavipes* and *B. lepidus* are on the wing in September and October. Similar species of other genera are likely to be seen throughout the summer. All are very small (5-7 mm) black to blackish-brown flies with transparent to brownish wings.

Male swarms of these terrestrial species can often be seen close to the ground in the vicinity of water, and in windy conditions they and paired males and females are often blown on to the water, where the trout seem inordinately fond of them. Although these small black flies are often seen on lakes and reservoirs, they are far more important to the river fly-fisher. In fact, a good artificial will often bring up a trout even when no naturals are on the water. There are many good **Black Gnat** artificials.

DRONE FLY
Eristalis tenax

The larva of this species is known as the rat-tailed maggot, and it is found in mud or decaying vegetation in shallow water. The adult is yellow and brown with two yellow bands around the abdomen and looks like a wasp, except that it has only two wings. It may be encountered occasionally on stillwater at any time during the summer when the females return to lay their eggs. The only known artificial is the **Grafham Drone Fly**.

157 Phantom Midge Pupa   **158** Phantom Midge (adult female)

REED SMUTS
Simulium spp

These exceedingly tiny flies, commonly referred to as Black Flies, are also known – and with good reason – as the Angler's Curse or Black Curse as they are so difficult to imitate. The species is an aquatic one found only in running water. The tiny larvae are attached in countless millions to the stems of water-weeds and during the summer, hardly a day passes without a hatch, when, despite the tiny size of the flies trout may sip them down all day long to the exclusion of all other species which may be hatching.

The Reed Smuts are rather like a miniature house-fly, black to dark-brown and with transparent wings. About 35 different species are known in the UK, and while a few may be as long as 5 mm, most are between 2-3 mm. My own pattern, the **Goddard Smut**, is now so successful that I use no other, although a host of other patterns is available.

PHANTOM FLY
Chaoborus spp

The various species of this fly are found only in stillwater, and the winged adults (**158**) are similar in size and appearance to the more common Buzzers (*Chironomids*). However, unlike these, they are seldom seen during the day, seeming to hatch during darkness, and they are therefore of little interest to the fly-fisher, except possibly in

159 Crane-fly
(Daddy-long- legs)

160 Gravel Bed Fly

late evening, when the females return to lay their eggs. The free-swimming, almost transparent larvae and pupae (**157**) are most useful to the stillwater fisher, as where they do occur, the trout certainly feed on them. This is usually in the shallower, shady areas. The only artificials are the **Phantom Larva** and **Phantom Pupa**, both by Peter Gathercole.

CRANE-FLY
Tipula spp

There are many different species in this genus, but only the larger species are of interest to fly-fishers, and these are so well known that a description is hardly necessary (**159**). These large, ungainly flies are often blown on to the water in late summer, and the trout certainly take them well enough, particularly on large lakes and reservoirs. There are many artificial Daddy patterns.

GRAVEL BED FLY
Hexatoma fuscipennis

This terrestrial species (**160**) closely related to the Crane-fly, is often found close to water, particularly on rivers with sandy or gravelly beds. It is commonest in the northern parts of the country. It is a dark-brownish-grey fly with two heavily-veined brownish wings, and it varies from 12-18 mm in length. Hatches, where they occur, are often prolific, and flies are blown on to or swarm over the water, dancing and dipping like Silverhorn Sedges. General patterns such as **Grey Duster** or **John Storey** must serve to imitate them, as no specific patterns exist.

COWDUNG FLY	OAK FLY
Corduleridae	*Rhagio Scolopacea*

Other *Diptera* often mentioned in old angling literature are the Cowdung Fly (**152**) and the Oak

Fly (**151**) or Downlooker as it was also called. However, I have never seen either of these on the water in sufficient quantities to interest the trout, so I tend to discount them and the many patterns from the past.

BLUEBOTTLE

One other seldom-mentioned common fly is the common Bluebottle. It is not often seen on the water, but I rate the artificial highly. Trout will often rise to it on rivers in late summer when little fly is on the water, and they do this even in quite deep pools, where they seem to be sulking on the bottom. Taff Price's **Bluebottle** is an excellent artificial.

Midges or Buzzers (*Chironomidae*)

This relatively large Family includes more than 430 different species. Many of these have terrestrial origins, so are of no interest to the fly-fisher, but a number do have aquatic life-cycles, and those species that occur in lakes and rivers form a staple diet for trout, particularly in stillwater. They vary tremendously in size, some of the larger species having a wing-length in excess of 8 mm, while the wings of some of the smaller species are barely one millimetre.

Hatches of these non-biting Midges, or Buzzers, are often on a huge scale on some of our large lakes and reservoirs, and as hardly a day goes by without the emergence of at least some species, it

161 Midge Larva
(Bloodworm)

162 Discarded
pupal case

is strange that they were considered of little consequence as angling flies until the middle of this century. Even today they are largely ignored on rivers, but they are now without doubt the most important Family of flies for the stillwater fisherman.

It was due largely to research by Dr Bell, of Blagdon, during the 1930s that they were brought to the attention of fly-fishers generally. Dr Bell perfected a pattern to represent the pupa as it hung in the surface film, and this he called his **Black Buzzer**. It was so successful that its fame spread far and wide, and it accounts for a lot of trout to this day.

163 Midge Pupa (early stage)　　**164** Golden Dun Midge Pupa

It was during the 1960s that I launched my own series of patterns which proved so successful. Although my dressing was based loosely on Dr Bell's, I believe I was the first to present a **Hatching Midge Pupa** pattern with a white tail to represent the whitish-coloured caudal fins and a bunch of white material pointing forward over the eye to represent the white tracheal gills on the naturals. These two important features are present on nearly all patterns that have been developed since.

Modern stillwater fly-fishers have a much better understanding of the importance of this fascinating Family, and as a result many new patterns have been developed and a high percentage of trout caught are taken on one type of Midge pattern or another. Despite this, most river fly-fishers are completely unaware of the importance of these flies in the ecology of running water, although it has been established that in the slower stretches of many rivers, including the chalk-streams, the smaller species of *Chironomidae* outnumber the *Ephemeroptera* by at least four to one. Perhaps more interest will be shown in them by river fly-fishers in the future.

166 Grey Boy Pupa hatching at surface (note orange colour of emerging wings which quickly fades.)

165 Grey Boy Midge Pupa

The celebrated French fly-fisherman, Raymond Rocher, has for many years been writing of the importance of these on European rivers, and has described the many successful midge patterns he uses. More recently, Timothy Benn has written several interesting and provocative articles on the research he has been undertaking along the same lines on rivers in the UK.

The larvae

These worm-like creatures (**161**) some of which are more than an inch long can be seen in various colours according to species. They vary from a pale olive to various shades of brown through to a startling shade of red which is due to haemoglobin in the blood of some of the larger species. They are usually found at depths of between 3 ft and 18 ft, where most species build tubes of mud or sand which are attached to stones, shells or the stems of plants, or sometimes buried in silt or mud. Some species are free-swimmers, while others often leave their burrows to feed, when trout feed upon them freely and may be taken on an appropriate artificial.

167 Large Green Midge
(female)

168 Large Red Midge
(male)

The pupae

While some species of midge have a yearly
life-cycle, many produce two, three or possibly
more generations during a season, but most of
their lives are spent in the larval form (**161**). The
pupal stage lasts but days, mostly between 36 and
72 hours. During this period, the pupa rapidly
develops within the larval case, changing shape
and colour in the process (**163**). When ecdysis is
complete, the mature pupa emerges from the
larval cuticle, or skin, a process which may take
several hours, and then, when conditions are right,
swims slowly to the surface, where the final
transformation into the winged adult takes place.

It is during this last stage of pupal life, as the
pupa swims to, or hangs beneath, the surface, that
it is most vulnerable to the depredations of the
trout. When at rest, the pupa is strongly curved and
the body slim, often strongly ribbed, with the
colours of the adult showing through, while the
head portion is quite bulbous where the wings,
thorax and legs have developed. The pupa has
prominent white tufts on top of its head, which are
in effect the tracheal gills, or breathing filaments.
At the end of the tapering body are whitish-
coloured caudal fins, or appendages, which facili-
tate swimming. While some smaller species hatch
during the day, most of the larger species hatch in
the evening or early morning.

As the hatch begins, so trout start feeding on the
pupae as they swim to the surface, but then, as the
hatch builds up, they nearly always transfer their

169 Large Red Midge
(female)

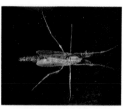

170 Grey Boy Midge
(male)

attention to the easier pickings just under the surface, where, unless it is windy and rough, the pupae will be hanging, unable to escape. A heavy surface rise of heading-and-tailing trout may always be anticipated on calm, windless mornings or evenings, as when the pupae reach the surface under these conditions, they nearly always have difficulty in penetrating the heavy surface film present in such conditions.

When they reach this film, the pupae rest briefly, hanging vertically. They then adopt a horizontal position and swim slowly along looking for a weakness in the film through which they can emerge. This film is often quite dense and it takes time for them to find a weak spot, so between periods of swimming, they return to the vertical position to rest, and the trout simply cruise along just under the surface, sipping them down.

It is at this time that my relatively new **Suspender Midge** patterns are exceptionally killing. Two or three of them are tied directly on to the leader and the little Ethafoam balls on their heads float

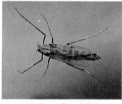

171 Grey Boy Midge
(female)

172 Golden Dun Midge
(male)

them in the film with their bodies hanging vertically, just like the natural. They should be cast into the path of a rising trout and left motionless apart from an occasional slow pull on the fly-line to tilt them horizontally like natural swimming pupae.

Good hatches of some of the smaller species can be expected on stillwaters at times during summer, and in breezy conditions the trout move directly upwind, sipping them down. However, in calm, windless conditions they usually rise erratically, often in circles.

The average size of *Chironomids* in most rivers is much smaller than that of those in the big lakes and reservoirs, but a tiny Suspender pattern (16 or 18) fished on its own on the point of the leader and in the surface film has recently proved to be an exceedingly effective method of catching any trout sipping down tiny flies on or just below the surface.

The adult

When a pupa breaks through the surface, it adopts a horizontal position (**182**) and within a matter of about 10 seconds the thorax splits (**166**) and the winged adult emerges, often resting on its own now-empty shuck for a second or so while its wings dry before it takes off. Emergence is often more rapid in rivers, where there is little or no surface film to impede the pupae.

Despite the many different species in this family, they are all similar apart from size. The females have stout, cylindrical bodies, while the males are often slim. Their bodies are usually a little longer than the transparent or slightly opaque wings,

173 Golden Dun Midge
(female)

174 Olive Midge
(male)

which lie flat, and slightly overlapping, along the top of their bodies while they are at rest.

They have six quite long legs but no tails, but they do have two antennae on top of their heads. These are quite short in the females, while in the males they are quite long and hairy or plumose. Most species are black, brown, green or various shades in between, though a few are red or reddish-orange. The body segments of some species are a different colour to the joints, which gives them a ribbed or banded appearance.

They are a common and abundant Family, and sometimes, particularly on stillwater, hatches are both prolonged and heavy. The males often form large swarms in early evening, and at times they can be seen in dense clouds even over the tops of tall trees, where they have the appearance of a column of smoke. Most stillwater anglers will be familiar with the egg-carrying, hook-shaped females which gyrate over the water at head-height, buzzing loudly (hence the fisherman's common name, Buzzer) before they dip down over the water to oviposit. Trout often take emerging adults and sometimes egg-laying females.

The following list of fisherman's Midges was compiled by myself for my book, *The Trout Flies of Stillwater*, in 1969. Before then no one had attempted to provide even a partial list, so it was left to me to suggest what I hoped would be acceptable

175 Blae and Black Midge(female)

176 Blae and Black Midge (male)

fisherman's names for most of the common species. By 1982, when my book, *Stillwater Flies: How and when to fish them*, was first published I had concluded that a few of the names were not generally acceptable, so in this volume I have published a new list and re-named those species that were in doubt. I have adhered to this new format for the adult Midges, but I must point out that the entomological names I have suggested (genus and species) are provided only as a guide to what seems to be the most common and widespread species of a particular size and colour.

THE ADULT MIDGES (*Chironomids*)

Angler's name	Entomological name	Wing-length
Large Green Midge	*Chironomus plumosus group*	6.5-8 mm
Large Red or Ginger Midge	*Chironomus plumosus group*	6.5-8 mm
Grey Boy (previously the Orange and Silver)	*Chironomus plumosus group*	6.5-8 mm
Golden Dun Midge	*Chironomus plumosus group*	6.5-8 mm
Olive Midge (previously the Ribbed Midge)	*Chironomus plumosus group*	6.5-7 mm
Blae and Black (previously the Black Midge)	*Chironomus anthracinus*	5-7.5 mm
Blagdon Green Midge	*Endochironomus albipennis*	4-6 mm
Small Brown Midge	*Glyptotendipes paripes*	4-6 mm
Small Red Midge	*Microtendipes pedellus*	4-4.5 mm
Small Black Midge	*Polypedilum nubeculosus*	3.5-4 mm

The Fly-fisher's Midges

LARGE GREEN MIDGE
Chironomus plumosus group

The largest of the Midges (8mm). The adult (**167**) has a dark green body with a pale-brown thorax and head with dark patches on either side. The legs are yellow-olive. The pupa is also dark green, with a dark thorax and brownish wing-cases, and is so large that the artificial should be dressed on a 12 or even a 10 hook. It is a common species on both Blagdon and Chew, emerging during late evening in July and August.

LARGE RED or GINGER MIDGE
Chironomus plumosus group

Another large species (8 mm), and one of the most handsome of all Midges. The adult (**168**) has a reddish-orange body and legs with a pale-orange-brown head. The pupa is dull red with a dark thorax and wing-cases. It is one of the least common of the Midges. Hatches are always sparse, often occurring during the day or early evening. The adults are most likely to be seen from July to September.

GOLDEN DUN MIDGE
Chironomus plumosus group

A medium-to-large species (7 mm). The adult (**172, 173**) has a lovely golden-olive body with brownish patches along the top of the body segments. The thorax and head are yellow with a distinctive black patch on either side. The legs are yellow-olive with touches of black. The pupa (**164**) has an olive-brown body with a pale-buff thorax and wing-cases. It is a common and widespread species, hatching in late evening or early morning from mid-summer onwards.

BLAGDON GREEN MIDGE
Endochironomus albipennis

This medium-to-small species (6 mm) is common on Blagdon, where it was first recognised. It is a fairly common species and the adult (**177**) may be recognised easily as it is the only small-sized midge with a bright-green body apart from *Chironomus viridis*, which is much smaller. This is another day-hatching species, but emergence during the day or early morning is often rather sparse. Adults are to be seen throughout the warmer summer months.

177 Blagdon Green Midge (male)

SMALL BROWN MIDGE
Glyptotendipes paripes

This is usually a little smaller (5 mm) than the Blagdon Green, and the adult (**178**) is dark-chestnut brown. It is a common and widespread species, and hatches, often heavy, usually begin

178 Small Brown Midge (male)

around mid-day and last to early evening during June and early July. However, hatches are at best sporadic.

SMALL RED MIDGE
Microtendipes pedullus

A rather small midge (6.5 mm). The adult (**179**, **180**) has a port-wine-red body with dark legs. It is a fairly common and widespread species, and another that hatches by day. Adults are more likely to be seen later in the summer than the Small Brown. Hatches tend to be sporadic.

179 Small Red Midge (female) **180** Small Red Midge (male)

SMALL BLACK MIDGE
Polypedilum nubeculosus

A very small species (3.5 mm). The adult (**181**) has a blackish body and legs with whitish wings. This and similar species are common and widespread, and hatches are often prolific during late evening

181 Small Black Midge (male)

or early morning during the latter half of the summer. The trout often become selective when feeding on these and are difficult to tempt. These small Midges and the Small Red and Brown Midges usually hatch in rivers during late evening.

GREY BOY
Chironomus plumosus group

Another medium-to-large species (7 mm). The adult (**171**, **172**) has a dark-silvery-grey body with reddish-orange ringing and a greyish thorax and head with touches of orange. The legs are orange-brown and the wings, when the adult first emerges, are often orange-brown. The pupa has a dark thorax, orange wing-cases and the body is bright-silver-grey, ringed with dark-reddish-orange – hence the original common name I bestowed. It is one of our most common and widespread species. Hatches, which are often prolific, occur during the day in April and early May and during evening, when the water temperature is high enough, from mid-May to mid-June.

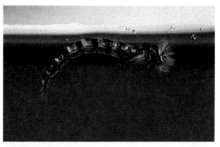

182 A Grey Boy Pupa about to hatch in surface film

OLIVE MIDGE
Chironomus plumosus group

A medium-sized species (7 mm), common and widespread. The adult (**174**) has a pale-olive-brown body distinctly ribbed with thick ivory-coloured bands, with a pale-brown thorax and head. The pupa has a body of similar colour, faintly ringed with ivory. The adults hatch in early morning or late evening and have quite a long season – May and June and August and September.

BLAE AND BLACK
Chironomus anthrancinus

This species is known as the Duck Fly or Harlequin Fly in parts of Wales and Scotland. It is a medium-sized (6.5 mm), all-black midge (**175**, **176**) and sometimes its transparent wings have a whitish tinge. Hatches occur during the day or early evening, and the main emergence is from March through early April, although adults (or those of similar species) may be seen throughout the summer.

Other Diptera

In addition to the prolific Midges, many other similar Families are found mostly in ponds, lakes and reservoirs, and there is little doubt that the trout feed upon the pupae of most of them, and probably the larvae and adults as well. However, little is known as yet about the potential of some of these Families from the fly-fisher's point of view. A few of the more common Families are:

CULCIDAE
This Family includes many species of mosquito and common gnat, the larvae and pupae of which are to be found in countless numbers in any stagnant or still water, from rainwater butts to the margins of large lakes.

TANYPODINAE
The adults are similar to some species of Midge, while the pupae are similar to those of the gnats,

having transparent bodies and brownish-coloured heads and thoraces. In stillwater they are to be found about mid-water, and, like the gnat pupae, they descend rapidly towards the bottom when disturbed.

CERATOPOGONIDAE

The flies of this Family are extremely small and include many of the biting midges, loosely termed Black Flies, which are often such a curse during the summer in many colder latitudes. The minute pupae may often be seen in countless numbers in stillwater. They have slender, segmented bodies with large bulbous heads.

DIXINAE

These are similar to the mosquitoes. There are two genera, the *Dixa*, found in running water, and the *Dixella*, associated with still or stagnant water. The adults are small with a body-length of less than 6 mm. Their heads are similar to those of the Midges, with three distinct dark stripes, but their bodies are slimmer and the wings longer than their bodies. The larvae of many of these species are like those of the mosquitoes, and will descend rapidly when disturbed. The pupae leave the water in a similar manner to those of the *Chironomidae*.

Artificials to Represent the Midges

The larvae of the midges are difficult to imitate with fur and feather as they swim with a figure-of-eight lashing movement. I can suggest only three artificials: my own **Red** or **Green Larva**; the **Bloodworm** (John Wilshaw); and the **Marabou Bloodworm** (Taff Price).

Of the three stages of interest to the fly-fisher, the pupal stage is the most important, and here there are plenty of artificials from which to choose. My recommendation is that the following patterns should be carried in various colours and sizes to match the naturals most likely to be hatching:

Hatching Midge pupa (Goddard); **Hatching Buzzer Pupa** (Collyer); **Marabou Midge Pupa** (Price); and the **Footballer** (Bucknall). But while all these are excellent patterns, my own preference is my own **Suspender Hatching Midge Pupa** during a heavy surface rise, while at other times, when trout are taking just below the surface, my favourite is Bob Carnill's **Poly-Rib C Pupa**. These may not be to everybody's taste as they are time-consuming to dress, but they are super-imitative patterns. An excellent general pattern is Dr Bell's **Grenadier**.

There is also a good choice of patterns to represent both the emerging or hatching adult and the fully-winged adult. These are, to my mind, less important, as the trout will take at least a dozen pupae for every adult taken. But these hatching and adult patterns should also be dressed in different colours and sizes. They are: **Adult Midge** (Richard Walker); **Emergent Midge** (Price); **Resting Midge** (Price); **Skating** or **Whirling Midge** (Price); **Black Midge** (Henderson); **Duck Fly** (J. R. Harris); and that good wet pattern, the traditional **Blae and Black**. My own preference is for Bob Carnill's series of **Adult Buzzers**, which are fished as wet flies just below the surface to represent dead, dying or drowned Midges, or to simulate the freshly-hatched adults struggling to become airborne.

CHAPTER EIGHT

Various Flies and Other Fauna

Ants, bees, wasps, beetles, bug, shrimps, moths

All the flies covered so far have been classified within definite Orders, with all Families and species in each Order having a similar life-cycle. However, so many other Orders contain just one or two species that are of interest to the fly-fisherman that it is impossible to deal with them Order by Order. In addition, many other small creatures, some aquatic, some terrestrial, do not come within the Class Insecta, but within completely different Classes. I shall deal with each of these flies or creatures separately, with a brief summary of their life-cycles given only where necessary. Some of them are of considerable importance to both trout and angler, while others are of interest only at certain times or under certain conditions.

ALDER FLY
Sialis lutaria or *S. fuliginosa*

The two genera are so similar that it is all but impossible to tell the difference, but only *S. lutaria* is found in stillwater. It is a common and widely-distributed fly, and the larvae are found in all types of water. They crawl ashore to pupate and adults are seen on the wing during May and June.

The larva (**184**) which is often more than an inch long is a fierce creature and strongly predaceous, often attacking and killing creatures larger than itself. It lives for much of its life in a tunnel formed in the silt or mud of the river or lake bed, and it is

183 Alder Fly (*Sialis lutaria* or *S. fuliginosa*)   **184** Alder Larva (*Sialis lutaria* or *S. fuliginosa*)

when it leaves this to feed or migrate shorewards to pupate that it makes a tempting target for a trout. The larva is dark-chestnut-brown on top and yellow or creamy-coloured beneath. Patterns to represent it are popular with stillwater anglers, but are seldom used on rivers.

The adult (**183**) has brown mottled-black roof-shaped wings and a dark-grey, almost black, body. It looks for all the world like a medium-sized Sedge-fly, but close examination will show that the wings are hard and shiny, unlike the wings of the Sedge-flies, which are soft and hairy.

The adults are of little account to fly-fishers, as, despite the fact that they are always flying and fluttering close to the water, they seldom land on it, and in all the years I have been fishing, I have seen very few taken by trout. One old and famous pattern called the **Alder Fly** even today accounts for a lot of trout on rivers, but I doubt that it is taken for an Alder. An Alder Larva pattern fished slowly near the bottom of lakes and reservoirs from early April to late May accounts for a lot of trout. There are several artificial patterns, but the best one I know is Stewart Canham's **Alder Larva**.

ANTS
Hymenoptera

Many creatures of terrestrial origin are blown on to the water, and trout, being opportunist feeders, take advantage of any offerings that are presented to them. Some are more favoured than others, among them the ants.

155

There are many species of ant – red, black, yellow – and they come in many sizes, but most have one thing in common: they grow wings during the mating season and become airborne, usually on hot, humid days in July and August. Then they are to be seen in their millions, and should any be near water on a windy day, then the rise of trout will be something to remember. Unfortunately, the occurrence is rather rare and few fly-fishers are prepared for it.

Many years ago, when I experienced my first fall of ants, I was unprepared, too, and I failed to take a trout during one of the biggest rises I have ever experienced. Since then, I have never been without a few ant patterns in my fly-box, and on the few occasions that I have been fishing during a fall of ants, I have been well rewarded.

It is essential to have a good imitative pattern, as trout on the ant will accept nothing else. A big brown wood ant reminds me of those old pictures of Victorian women – large chests and hips, and tiny waists – and unless an artificial is dressed in the same manner, it will certainly not attract the trout. Many dressings are available, but one of the oldest – Skues' **Dusky Wood** – is, in my opinion, as good as any.

BEES AND WASPS
Hymenoptera

Bees and wasps are well-enough known not to need description. They are of doubtful value to the fly-fisher, but occasionally one is blown on to the water and seems to be accepted readily enough by the trout. I normally carry just one yellow-and-black striped pattern in my fly-box – just in case.

BEETLES
Coleoptera

More than 3,000 species of beetle are known, making the *Coleoptera* one of the largest Orders of all living creatures. Despite this, they have received little recognition in angling literature. This is strange, since more than 220 species have an aquatic origin. The probable explanation is that few of them are common and abundant, and even those that are like the cover of heavy weed, so the fisherman is probably unaware of them, although the trout undoubtedly feed on them at times. While terrestrial species are in the majority, relatively few are seen near water and are recognised by anglers. They include:

COCH-Y-BONDDU
Phyllopertha horticola

(**185**) This quite small beetle, about ½ inch long, has a metallic bluish-green head and thorax with a black body and reddish-brown wings. It is most likely to be encountered in parts of Scotland and Wales, often in large swarms during warm days in June. In some areas it is also known as the June Bug or Bracken Clock. It is sometimes blown on to the water, providing a feast for the trout. An old but excellent traditional representative pattern is called the **Coch-y-bonddu**.

185 Coch-y-bonddu

COCKCHAFER
Melolontha melolontha

This beetle (**186**) belongs to the same family as the Coch-y-bonddu, but is much larger. It is, in fact, one of our largest terrestrial beetles, with a body-length often exceeding 25 mm. The head and thorax are black, the body is banded with black and grey, and the wings are reddish-brown. It is common and fairly widespread, appearing singly or in small swarms during May and June, but it is seldom seen in Southern England. Its large size makes it of doubtful value to the fly-fisher, as the trout seem rather wary of it. It is on the wing in the evening when, in windy conditions, it is often blown on to the water. The only known pattern is the **Cockchafer** (Henderson).

186 Cockchafer Beetle   **187** Soldier Beetle

SOLDIER BEETLE
Cantharis rustica

Most fly-fishers must be aware of this common beetle (**187**) which can be seen flying around bankside herbage during June, July and August. A slim species a little over ½ inch long, it is conspicuous by its bright-orange-red wings and yellowish body. An artificial is Skues' **Soldier Beetle**.

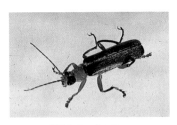

188 Sailor Beetle

SAILOR BEETLE
Cantharis lividia

The Sailor Beetle (**188**) has the same habitat as the Soldier Beetle, but is not quite so common. It is similar in appearance except that the wings are dull blue and the body is reddish-orange. It is of little account to the fly-fisher, at least in the southern part of the country, although it may be of more importance on northern waters where fly-life is more at a premium. Trout occasionally take it when it is blown on to the water. An artificial is Taff Price's **Sailor Beetle**.

GROUND BEETLES

Countless species of ground beetle sometimes crawl or are blown on to the water. Most are dark-coloured and vary greatly in size and are accepted by the trout readily enough when in sufficient numbers. Many species of leaf beetle often fall on to water from overhanging trees, and trout lie in wait for them. Such beetles are quite small, usually less than 10 mm long, and the most common are metallic-blue or green.

AQUATIC BEETLES

The many aquatic species of this Order are probably of more interest to trout as, where they occur, they are available on a more permanent basis in both larval and adult forms. However, few, if any, of these aquatic species are found in open water. They seem to prefer a habitat of heavy weed or pockets therein, and so the trout have to seek them out. This is probably why they have been largely ignored by fly-fishers, as it is virtually impossible to work an artificial fly among heavy weed. Apart from this, many of these aquatic species are either uncommon or only locally distributed. Of the few that are common and widespread the best known are as follows:

GREAT DIVING BEETLE
Dytiscus spp

This is probably the best-known of the diving beetles (**190**). It is found in stillwater and its larva (**189**), which often attains a length of nearly 2 inches, is carnivorous and ferocious. The adult is about 1¼ inches long and olive-brown with yellow margins on the wing-cases.

189 Beetle Larva (probably   **190** Male Diving Beetle
Dytiscus spp)   (*Dytiscus*)

GREAT SILVER BEETLE
Dytiscus spp

This is one of our best-known aquatic beetles, but, sadly, it seems to be on the decline and is now found mainly in the southern parts of England, where it occurs in both stillwater and slow streams. It is one of the largest members of the Order and often reaches a length of 1¾ inches. The adult is greenish-black and is more likely to be seen crawling or browsing on the weed rather than swimming. It is unusual to see more than one at a time.

WHIRLIGIG BEETLES
Gyrinus spp

This family has 10 species, all somewhat similar. The larvae are slender creatures about 1 inch long with long, thin tracheal gills extending from the body segments down each side. The adults (**191**) are dark-coloured, often black, and quite small,

191 Whirligig Beetle
(*Gyrinus Spp*)

192 Semi-aquatic Beetle
(*Donacia*)

rarely exceeding 10 mm in length. They will often
be seen in considerable numbers during August
and September in clear patches among weed-
beds, gyrating madly around one another. I have
often seen trout taking them along the margins.

Other semi-aquatic beetles likely to be seen are
the various species of *Donacia* (**192**). These bright
metallic beetles are found on waterside vegetation.

ROVE or STAPH BEETLES
Staphylinoidea

This is one of the largest Families of *Coleoptera*,
containing nearly 1,000 different species. Many
members of the Family are a shiny-black colour
and most are slim. Some of the smaller species are
barely 3 mm long. They are strong fliers, but are
often blown on to the water during May and June
and again in September. Some members of the
Family have a distinctly orange thorax, and Taff
Price has perfected an excellent pattern based on
this colour which he calls the **Rove Beetle**.

ARTIFICIAL BEETLES

Despite the many varieties of beetle, few imitative
patterns have been devised other than those
mentioned for a few of the species described.
However, quite a few general patterns are available, the best of them being: **Eric's Beetle**
(Horsfall-Turner); **Black and Peacock Spider**
(Ivens); and **Black Ground Beetle** (Price).

DAPHNIA

These tiny creatures are important to the stillwater fly-fisher as they form a staple diet for trout. They are too tiny to be imitated individually, but they congregate in huge clouds and trout feeding on them can often be caught on other types of artificial. The clouds of daphnia are influenced by light. On dull, cloudy days they are most likely to be found fairly close to the surface, but on bright, sunny days they are more likely to be found in the deepest areas of a lake or reservoir.

DRAGONFLIES
Odonata

Every angler must be familiar with these large, brilliantly-coloured insects and the similar damselflies. The dragonflies are by far the larger of the two Families. They have stout bodies and two pairs of wings of unequal length which they hold open when at rest. The damselflies are slimmer-bodied and have wings of equal length which are always closed over their bodies when they are at rest. Adult dragonflies are of no interest to the fly-fisher as they seldom approach the water surface.

Dragonfly nymphs (**193**, **194**), which are aquatic and can attain a length of nearly 2 inches, are fearsome creatures. They are carnivorous and will attack even small fish when opportunity occurs. Artificials to represent them have been devised, but as they seem to prefer the cover of heavy

193 Large Dragonfly Nymph

194 Large Dragonfly Nymph about to transpose

weed, trout seldom have the opportunity to feed on them and they are of doubtful value to the angler.

DAMSELFLIES
Zygoptera

These slim, elegant-looking flies occur in various colours, with red, green, brown and blue predominant. There are 17 British species in this Family, of which the two most common are *Agrion splendens*, which seems to prefer running water, and *Enallagma cyathigerum*, more likely to be seen on big lakes and reservoirs. The male of *A. splendens* has a vivid metallic-green body (**195**), while the female has a brownish body. The male of *E. cyathigerum* has a brilliant-blue body (**196**), while the female is a dull-greenish colour (**197**).

195 Green Damselfly (male) (*Agrion splendens*)   **196** Blue Damselfly (male) (*Enallagama cyathigarum*)

197 Green-bodied Damselfly (female)

The adults may be of interest to the fly-fisher at times, as before mating they fly low over the water surface and during mating the coupled flies land on any convenient emergent vegetation, down which the females eventually crawl to lay their eggs underwater. Trout often feed on the females as they return to the surface, and I have on many occasions seen trout leap out of the water and take a damselfly in the air.

Many fly-dressers have attempted to create imitative patterns, but the only one I know that has proved consistently successful is Stewart Canham's **Damselfly**.

198 Damselfly Nymph –
Brown

199 Damselfly Nymph –
Green

The nymphs of the damselflies (**198**, **199**) are, like the adults, very slim. They are adept at camouflage and take on the colour of their main habitat, so they are likely to be seen in colours ranging from pale brown to deep green. They live in weed, moss or silt on the bottom. While they are found in rivers, they are largely ignored by river fly-fishers. However, they are important in still-water, and patterns to imitate them carry out great execution.

When the nymphs are ready to transform into adults, they swim towards the shore just beneath the surface with a distinctive wriggling motion, making tempting targets for trout, which often take them savagely. This shoreward migration usually occurs in the morning, when conditions are right, at any time from the middle of June to late August. Many good imitative patterns have been devised, but in my opinion the best is Cliff Henry's **Damsel Nymph** or my own **Damsel Wiggle Nymph**.

FRESHWATER LOUSE
Asellus aquaticus, A. meridianus

Also known in some areas as the Water Hoglouse, or Water Slater (**200**), this is a common and widespread species found in all types of stillwater. It is a *Crustacean*, 10-12 mm long, and similar in size and colour to the Freshwater Shrimp, with which it is often found. It is abundant in detritus or mud, mostly in the shallow water of the margins of ponds, lakes and even some of the larger reservoirs. It is a rather lethargic creature and difficult to imitate. It does not seem particularly well-liked by trout, and it is seldom found during an autopsy, although it is possibly accepted more readily in winter when other insect life is scarce. There are only a few artificial patterns known, of which Peter Lapsley's **Freshwater Louse** is the best and certainly the easiest to dress.

200 Freshwater Louse   **201** Freshwater Shrimp

FRESHWATER SHRIMPS
Gammarus spp

These small crustaceans (**201**) reach an average size of 12-14 mm and are a translucent pale-watery colour. They are extremely common, abundant and widespread, but of several species, the two most common are probably *Gammarus pulex* and *G. lacustris*.

Although they are often found with the Freshwater Louse, they seem to prefer a habitat of weed or moss rather than mud. They are found in both stillwater and in most rivers. They are probably of more value to the fly-fisher in running water, as river trout can constantly be seen feeding on them, scooping them out of the gravel or moss with the sides of their mouths. When the fish are so engaged, a weighted shrimp pattern can be deadly.

They are not so readily available to trout in lakes and reservoirs as they are usually confined to the shallower margins. Consequently, they do not often occur in autopsies during summer, but in winter, when other insect life is scarce, they do provide a valuable source of food. Many artificials have been devised to represent these crustaceans, but two popular and effective patterns are my own or Brian Clarke's **Mating Shrimp** and Neil Patterson's **Red Spot Shrimp**. My own **Gerroff** is also worth trying in slow or shallow water.

GRASSHOPPERS

There are several species of this well-known insect and in bygone days they were doubtless a valuable source of food for trout when blown on to the water. Unfortunately, they are now of little or no consequence, as they have largely been wiped out along the river banks by agricultural pesticides. No doubt trout still accept them in areas where they do occur in sufficient numbers, but Hopper artificials are no longer available in this country. However, there are many excellent American patterns and they are widely used in the USA.

WATER BUGS
Hemiptera

This Order includes many different Families, and the bugs are found in many shapes and sizes. Some live on the surface, while others live beneath it. Most are common and widespread, and most are found in or on stillwater, although some are also found in slower sections of running water.

LESSER WATER BOATMAN
Corixa

These small beetle-like creatures (**202**) are found
only in weedy areas of stillwater, and as they have
to make constant journeys to the surface to
replenish their oxygen supply, they seldom live in
water more than 3 ft deep. The species is
important to the fly-fisherman as on most stillwaters
the trout will move into the shallows to feed on
them, usually during August and September when
other forms of food are rather scarce, or perhaps
because this is the time of year at which *Corixae*
take to the wing during mating and move around.
The 31 British species vary in size from a little
under 5 mm to a little over 12 mm. Many excellent
imitative patterns are available, dressed either
weighted or unweighted. The pattern shown in the
colour section is my recommendation.

202 Corixa or Lesser Water Boatman

GREATER WATER BOATMAN or
BACKSWIMMER
Notonecta

This is similar to the Lesser Water Boatman except
that it is much larger and spends most of its time
swimming upside-down in the surface film, hunting
for food (**203**). It is of doubtful value to the angler
as, although it is quite common, it seldom seems to

be taken by trout. No well-known artificial represents it, but a large unweighted **Corixa** pattern should suffice.

203 Greater Water Boatman, and its reflection in the mirror

COMMON WATER BUG
Aphelocheirus montandoni, Ilyocoris cimicoides

A few closely-allied species of round or oval-shaped water bug are mostly brownish and can be found swimming in weedy areas. They are undoubtedly taken by trout on occasion. Most are fairly small except for these two more common species. *A montandoni* (**204**) is about 10 mm long, and *I. cimicoides* about 15 mm. I know of no artificials.

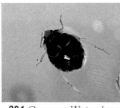

204 Common Water-bug
(*Aphelocheirus montandoni*)

205 Water Measurer
Hydrometra

POND SKATERS and WATER MEASURERS

Apart from the fully aquatic species, there are two Families of Water Bug which include many species that spend all their lives on the water surface. These are the Pond Skaters and Water Measurers (**205**). Most of them are stillwater or stagnant-water species, but although they are common on most trout ponds or lakes, they seldom leave the shelter of the banks or shallow margins. They are therefore not readily available to the trout and not generally of much interest to the fly-fisher. I know of no artificials to represent them, although I am sure the trout would take any that came within range.

LACEWINGS
Neuroptera

These beautiful insects have wonderful golden eyes and transparent gauzy wings which reflect all the colours of the rainbow. They are closely related to the Alder Fly and are of a similar size and shape, often exceeding ¾ inch in length.

Although more than 50 different species are known, they are of doubtful value to the fly-fisher as they are strictly terrestrial. However, they do seem to have an affinity for water and are sometimes blown on to the surface in considerable numbers. The trout can then often become very selective. Twice in recent years I have experienced a good evening fall of these flies, once on the Itchen and once on the Kennet, and on each occasion the trout picked out the lacewings in preference to other flies.

206 Green Lacewing

GREEN LACEWING
Chrysopidae

The Green Lacewing (**203**) is probably the most common and, with its brilliant-green body, is certainly the prettiest. The artificial I recommend is Taff Price's **Green Lacewing**.

LEECHES
Hirudinae

The 16 British species vary greatly in size, from about 10 mm up to nearly 100 mm. While a few species are almost transparent, most are greenish to brown, while some are greyish to black. They can often be seen either looping their way along the bottom or on waterweed. Sometimes they may be seen in open water, as they are excellent swimmers. Although some species may be found in rivers, they are of little account to the river fly-fisher. However, in stillwaters they are important, as the trout are rather partial to them and a free-swimming leech makes a tempting target. This is without doubt one of the reasons that lures are so effective on many of our large lakes and reservoirs.

The leech is a long, worm-like creature with a sucker at each end. The one at the head contains the mouth parts. Its free-swimming movement is undulating. Marabou is an excellent material for simulating this, so I thoroughly recommend an artificial called the **Marabou Leech** (Taff Price). Another pattern I would suggest is the **Black Bear's Hair Lure** (Cliff Henry). Tied correctly, this also swims with a distinctive undulating motion.

MOTHS
Lepidoptera

This large Order of insects boasts more than 2,000 British species. Despite this, they are of little interest to either fly-fisher or trout. Most moths are nocturnal and those that live close to water do occasionally end up on the surface, usually in late evening. Yet it is seldom that one is seen being taken by a trout, on either stillwater or running water. That being so, it is difficult to understand why they were considered a useful addition to the fly-fisher's armoury in the past. A few Families are of interest.

BROWN CHINA MARK MOTHS
Nymphula nympheata, N. stratiotata

Several species of aquatic moth (rather like the Caddis-flies) have larvae and, in some cases, pupae, that live underwater. The most common of these are the Brown China Mark Moths, of which the species *Nymphula nympheata* (**208**) is the most widely distributed. A slightly larger species, *Nymphula stratiotata* (**207**), is less common and is found only in southern England. The adults may be seen on the wing among the waterside vegetation around ponds and lakes during June and July.

207 Aquatic China Mark Moth

208 China Mark Moth with wings spread

SMALL WHITE AQUATIC MOTH
Acentroupus niveus

This tiny white moth, with a wing-span of barely 8 mm, was named by Taff Price. There are two types of female, one which can fly and one with wings so tiny that it is incapable of flight. This remains underwater where it is able to swim. The adults are most likely to be seen during hot weather in July and August.

GHOST or SWIFT MOTHS
Family *Hepialidae*

This terrestrial species is quite large and has rather narrow whitish wings. It can be seen on the wing from June to July.

WAINSCOTT MOTHS
Genera *Leucania* and *Nonagria*

Another terrestrial species often seen close to water, as its pupae are found in hollow reed stems in the margins. It is thick-set, variable in size, and of a drab yellow to gingery-brown colour. It has a wing-span of about 16 mm and is common and widespread. It is to be seen from June to August.

WATER ERMINE
Spilosoma urticae

This medium-sized terrestrial white moth is seen only late at night, often in the vicinity of bankside vegetation. It has a wing-span of about 18 mm and its soft ermine-white wings are often covered in small black spots. It is most common in June.

ARTIFICIAL MOTH PATTERNS

Many moth patterns have been devised, some of them dating back to the last century, but few are now available commercially. The most popular patterns are: the **Ermine Moth**, the **Hoolet Moth** (G. Bucknall) and the **Ghost Swift Moth** (R. Walker). The **Grey Duster**, tied in different sizes, is a good general pattern to use when moths are about.

SPIDERS
Araneae

Unlike the insects, which have three pairs of legs and a body which is divided into three parts, head, thorax and abdomen, the spiders have four pairs of legs and a body divided into only two parts, head and abdomen.

Although this is a large Order, few of the spiders are of much value to the angler, as only a few Families are normally found near water. Of these, the following may be of some interest, as trout will certainly accept them on those few occasions when they do become available.

WOLF SPIDERS
Family *Lycosidae*

These are hunting spiders and are quite common along the shores of lakes and ponds, although some species prefer rivers and streams. They spin vertical silken tubes among the weed or moss in which they live. Much of their hunting is done on the water surface, where at times they may become available to the trout. They are not large, averaging about 8 mm in length.

209 Aquatic Spider and its bubble nest

RAFT SPIDERS
Genera *Dolomedes*

Another Family of spiders that live on the floating leaves of water-plants and hunt their prey by running along the water surface are known as Raft Spiders and belong to the Genera *Dolomedes*. They are among the largest of all the British spiders and vary between 15 mm and 20 mm in length.

PIRATE SPIDERS
Genera *Pirata*

Another Family of spiders that live among the water-weeds and hunt on the surface belong to the Genera *Pirata*. They are commonly called Pirate Spiders and vary between 5 mm and 8 mm.

WEB SPIDER
Genera *Tetragnatha*

One other Family worthy of mention belongs to the Genera *Tetragnatha*. These rather slim-looking spiders average about 10 mm and often spin their webs close to or even over the water surface. They are occasionally taken by trout when they are blown on to the surface.

AQUATIC SPIDER
Argyronata aquatica

This is one species that actually does live beneath the water surface (**210**). While this choice of habitat makes this creature unique among spiders, it is also unusual for another reason: it is one of the few species of spider in which the male is larger than the female and so is not eaten by her after mating.

This species not only hunts its prey beneath the surface (**211**), but to save frequent trips to the surface to replenish its oxygen supply, constructs

210 Aquatic Spider
Argyroneta aquatica

211 Aquatic Spider with
captured Water-louse

an airtight silken mantle attached to the weeds. (**209**). This is duly filled with air from the surface so that the spider can live underwater for considerable periods. The species has been largely ignored by fly-dressers, and the only two authors, Colonel Joscelyn Lane and Leonard West, have suggested dressings. However, so far as I am aware, none of the patterns is now available. The many so-called spider dressings are not intended to represent these insects, but merely illustrate a method of dressing popular among North Country fly-dressers.

WATER-MITES

These tiny, brightly-coloured creatures belong, like the spiders, to the Order *Arachnidae*. They are most likely to be seen in ponds and lakes, either swimming or clambering about among the water-plants. They are similar to small spiders, except that their bodies are not divided into two parts.

More than 200 species are known, but most of them are too tiny to interest trout. However, some of the larger species do grow to about 8 mm, and I have on occasion found them in the stomachs of trout. Most of them are round or oval-shaped and brightly coloured, with red predominating. Other colours are green and blue. One of the largest and most common is a bright-red species called *Hydrachna geographica* (**212**). This may be worth imitating with an artificial when it is seen, usually in the latter half of the summer. Richard

212 Water Mite (probably *Hydrachna*)

Walker devised a pattern to represent it which he called **The Red Mite**, and which had some success.

SNAILS

Many different species of aquatic snail are common to both stillwater and running water, and there is little doubt that they provide gourmet fare for trout. In fact, at times during the summer some trout seem to feed on them almost exclusively for quite long periods. These fish, when caught, have bulging stomachs, and if they are pressed a crunching sound can be heard as partly-digested shells collapse. Of the many species, those mostly likely to be seen are:

GREAT POND SNAIL

This is similar to a whelk and often attains a length in excess of 60 mm. It is by far the largest of the aquatic species.

EAR SNAIL

This has a preference for highly-alkaline water and is common in the southern counties. It often reaches a length of 30 mm.

GREAT RAMSHORN SNAIL and SMALL WHITE RAMSHORN
Planorbis corneus and *Planorbis albus*

The Great Ramshorn is whorl-shaped and reaches a length of about 25 mm. The Small White Ramshorn is one of the smallest species and rarely exceeds about 6 mm.

WANDERING SNAIL

Probably the most common species, this is often present in huge numbers in some of our larger lakes and big reservoirs, where it often reaches a length of more than 20 mm.

While snails form an important part of the trout's diet in both stillwater and running water, they are of no interest to the fly-fisher when the fish are browsing upon them among the weeds. However, they can be very important at times during the summer when a certain phenomenon occurs.

Most species found in stillwater have the dual ability to absorb oxygen either through their skins or direct from the atmosphere, and in late summer, when many stillwaters become slightly de-oxygenated, these snails float to the surface to replenish their oxygen supply. At such times it is possible to take the occasional trout on an imitative artificial fished in the surface film. On other rare occasions, too, practically every snail in a water seems to rise to the surface and float around, often for several days. The angler who is aware of this and has an appropriate pattern will have a field day.

Lack of oxygen may not be the only factor involved in this mass-migration of snails to the surface. In my experience the species most likely to be involved is the Wandering Snail, so an alternative explanation may be that it is a demonstration of migratory or mating behaviour peculiar to this species.

A trout feeding on floating snails takes them with a pronounced head-and-tail rise. This is typical also of a trout feeding on Midge Pupae, so it is easy to be fooled. Snails floating in the surface film cannot be seen by looking across the water surface, so when in doubt it pays to wade out as far as possible and look directly down into the surface. If snails are there, then they will be visible.

Several artificials are available, but I think that the original dressing perfected by Cliff Henry, which he called the **Floating Snail**, is the best.

STICKLEBACKS and FRY

Trout, particularly stillwater trout, are strongly predatory and will feed avidly on sticklebacks, the fry of other fish, and even on immature trout whenever opportunity occurs. The peak fry-feeding period is in the latter half of the summer, when the young fish leave the comparative safety of the shallow margins and heavy weed-beds to forage further afield. At this time a lure or fry pattern retrieved fairly fast close to the bank, or along the front edge of any bank of weed, often takes larger-than-average trout.

Trout foraging for fry can also often be seen as they make repeated incursions into shallow water after shoals of small fish. They often cause quite a disturbance on the surface as they slash through the shoals, and masses of fry may be seen jumping out of the water in their efforts to escape. Trout so engaged are surprisingly regular in their incursions, and it pays to time their movements and to present a lure to coincide with their return.

Many excellent lure or fry imitative patterns have been devised, of which these are a few of the best: **Polystickle**; **Sinfoil's Fry**; **Church Fry**; and **Mylar Minnow** (Brock). If a traditional pattern is preferred then I recommend a **Peter Ross**.

SAWFLY
Hymenoptera

These terrestrial flies (**213**), belonging to the same Order as the bees and wasps, are sometimes

213 Saw Fly (*Hymenoptera*)

blown on to the water. They are mostly dark-bodied, often with touches of yellow or orange. Several different species are included under the common name of Sawfly, among them the **Poplar Sawfly**, the **Pine Sawfly**, and the **Solomon's Seal Sawfly**. I know of no artificial to represent them.

TADPOLE

Everyone is familiar with this greeny-black creature that is the immature stage of the frog. Trout take them when they are available, and a pattern such as my own **Tadpolly** is often effective.

Emergence charts for the more common species of fly

April

Common name	Type of fly	Type of water	Size	Period of hatch
Sepia Dun	Upwinged	Still	Medium-large	Day
Large Brook Dun	Upwinged	Running	Large	Day
March Brown	Upwinged	Running	Large	Day
Large Dark Olive	Upwinged	Running	Medium-large	Day
Grannom	Sedge	Running	Medium	Day
Large Stonefly	Stonefly	Stony rivers, stony lakes	Very large	Day
February Red	Stonefly	Slow rivers	Medium	Day
Early Brown	Stonefly	Fast rivers	Medium	Day
Small Yellow Sally	Stonefly	Stony rivers	Small	Day
Hawthorn Fly	Flat-winged	Terrestrial	Large	Day
Grey Boy Midge	Flat-winged	Still	Medium	Day
Blae and Black Midge	Flat-winged	Still	Medium to small	Day

May

Common name	Type of fly	Type of water	Size	Period of hatch
Turkey Brown	Upwinged	Running	Medium-large	Day
Claret Dun	Upwinged	Still or slow	Medium-large	Day
Sepia Dun	Upwinged	Still	Medium-large	Day
Mayfly	Upwinged	Still or running	Very large	Day
Large Brook Dun	Upwinged	Running	Large	Day
Olive Upright	Upwinged	Stony rivers	Medium-large	Day
Black Sedge	Sedge	Running	Medium	Late Day
Large Stonefly	Stonefly	Stony rivers, stony lakes	Very large	Day
Early Brown	Stonefly	Fast rivers	Very large	Day
Small Yellow Sally	Stonefly	Stony rivers	Small	Day
Hawthorn	Flat-winged	Terrestrial	Large	Day
Grey Boy Midge	Flat-winged	Still	Medium	Day, evening
Alder Fly	Group 5	All types	Medium-large	Day

June

Common name	Type of fly	Type of water	Size	Period of hatch
Turkey Brown	Upwinged	Running	Medium-large	Day
Claret Dun	Upwinged	Still or slow	Medium-large	Day
Mayfly	Upwinged	Still or running	Very large	Day
Blue-winged Olive	Upwinged	Running, still	Medium-large	Mostly evening
Large Brook Dun	Upwinged	Running	Large	Day
Large Summer Dun	Upwinged	Still or slow	Very large	Day
Olive Upright	Upwinged	Stony rivers	Medium-large	Day
Large Spurwing	Upwinged	Running	Medium-large	Day
Caenis	Upwinged	All types	Very small	Day
Great Red Sedge	Sedge	Still or slow	Very large	Late day
Large Cinnamon	Sedge	Rivers, lakes	Large	Evening
Brown Sedge	Sedge	All types	Medium-large	Evening
Welshman's Button	Sedge	Rivers, lakes	Medium-large	Late day
Longhorns	Sedge	Still	Medium	Late day
Black Sedge	Sedge	Running	Medium	Late day

Brown and Black Silverhorns	Sedge	All types	Medium	Late day
Grousewing	Sedge	Still	Medium	Late day
Large Stonefly	Stonefly	Stony waters	Very large	Day
Small Yellow Sally	Stonefly	Stony rivers	Small	Day
Golden Dun Midge	Flat-winged	Still	Medium	Morning and evening
Olive Midge	Flat-winged	Still	Medium	Morning and evening
Small Brown Midge	Flat-winged	All types	Small	Day and evening
Small Black Midge	Flat-winged	All types	Very small	Morning or evening
Coch-y-bonddu	Beetle	Terrestrial	Medium-large	Day
Damselflies and nymphs	Group 5	All types	Very large	Day

July

Blue-winged Olive	Upwinged	Running, still	Medium-large	Mostly evening
Large Summer Dun	Upwinged	Still or slow	Very large	Day
Olive Upright	Upwinged	Stony rivers	Medium-large	Day
Small Dark Olive	Upwinged	Running	Very small	Day
Caenis	Upwinged	All types	Very small	Day
Great Red Sedge	Sedge	Still or slow	Very large	Late day

Common name	Type of fly	Type of water	Size	Period of hatch
Large Cinnamon	Sedge	Rivers, lakes	Large	Evening
Brown Sedge	Sedge	All types	Medium-large	Evening
Welshman's Button	Sedge	Rivers, lakes	Medium-large	Late day
Longhorns	Sedge	Still	Medium	Late day
Brown and Black Silverhorns	Sedge	All types	Medium	Late day
Grousewing	Sedge	Still	Medium	Late day
Yellow-spotted Sedge	Sedge	Still or slow	Medium to small	Late day
Large Green Midge	Flat-winged	Still	Medium	Morning, evening
Golden Dun Midge	Flat-winged	Still	Medium	Morning, evening
Small Brown Midge	Flat-winged	All types	Small	Day, evening
Small Red Midge	Flat-winged	All types	Small	Day, evening
Small Black Midge	Flat-winged	All types	Very small	Morning, evening
Damselflies and nymphs	Group 5	All types	Very large	Day
Snails	Group 5	Mostly still	Variable	Day

184

August

Blue-winged Olive	Upwinged	Running, still	Medium-large	Mostly evening
Autumn Dun	Upwinged	Stony waters	Large	Day
Large Summer Dun	Upwinged	Still or slow	Very large	Day
Small Dark Olive	Upwinged	Running	Very small	Day
Caenis	Upwinged	All types	Very small	Day
Caperer	Sedge	Running	Very large	Late day
Large Cinnamon	Sedge	Rivers, lakes	Large	Evening
Welshman's Button	Sedge	Rivers, lakes	Medium-large	Late day
Longhorns	Sedge	Still	Medium	Late day
Brown and Black Silverhorns	Sedge	All types	Medium	Late day
Grousewing	Sedge	Still	Medium	Late day
Yellow-spotted Sedge	Sedge	Still or slow	Medium to small	Late day
Willow Fly	Stonefly	Running	Medium-large	Day
Needle Fly	Stonefly	All types	Small	Day
Heather Fly	Flat-winged	Terrestrial	Large	Day

185

Common name	Type of fly	Type of water	Size	Period of hatch
Crane-fly	Flat-winged	Terrestrial	Very large	Day
Large Green Midge	Flat-winged	Still	Medium	Morning, evening
Golden Dun Midge	Flat-winged	Still	Medium	Morning, evening
Olive Midge	Flat-winged	Still	Medium	Morning, evening
Small Red Midge	Flat-winged	All types	Small	Day, evening
Small Black Midge	Flat-winged	All types	Very small	Morning, evening
Damselflies and nymphs	Group 5	All types	Very large	Day
Snails	Group 5	Mostly still	Variable	Day
Sticklebacks and fry	Group 5	Mostly still	Variable	Day
September				
Autumn Dun	Upwinged	Stony waters	Large	Day
Caperer	Sedge	Running	Large	Late day
Large Cinnamon	Sedge	Rivers, lakes	Large	Evening
Brown Sedge	Sedge	All types	Medium-large	Evening
Longhorns	Sedge	Still	Medium	Late day

Grousewing	Sedge	Still	Medium	Late day
Yellow-spotted Sedge	Sedge	Still or slow	Medium to small	Late day
Willow Fly	Stonefly	Running	Medium-large	Day
Needle Fly	Stonefly	All types	Small	Day
Heather Fly	Flat-winged	Terrestrial	Large	Day
Crane-fly	Flat-winged	Terrestrial	Very large	Day
Olive Midge	Flat-winged	Still	Medium	Day, evening
Small Black Midge	Flat-winged	All types	Very small	Morning, evening
Sticklebacks and fry	Group 5	Mostly still	Variable	Day

Species likely to be seen in most months

Common name	Type of fly	Type of water	Size	Period of hatch
Yellow May Dun	Upwinged	Rivers, lakes	Medium-large	Day
Medium Olive Dun	Upwinged	Running	Medium	Day
Pale Watery Dun	Upwinged	Running	Small	Day
Iron Blue Dun	Upwinged	Running	Small	Day
Small Spurwing	Upwinged	Rivers, lakes	Medium	Day
Pond Olive Dun	Upwinged	Still	Medium	Day
Lake Olive Dun	Upwinged	Still	Medium	Day
Pale Evening Dun	Upwinged	Slow rivers	Medium	Evening
Mottled Sedge	Sedge	Still	Large	Late day
Cinnamon Sedge	Sedge	All types	Medium-large	Late day
Medium Sedge	Sedge	All types	Medium	Late day
Sandfly	Sedge	Rivers	Medium	Late day
Small Red Sedge	Sedge	Still or slow	Medium to small	Late day
Small Yellow Sedge	Sedge	Running	Small	Evening
Yellow Sally	Stonefly	All types	Medium-large	Day
Small Brown	Stonefly	Slow rivers	Small	Day

Black Gnat	Flat-winged	Terrestrial	Medium to small	Day
Reed Smut	Flat-winged	Running	Very small	Day
Blagdon Green Midge	Flat-winged	Still	Small	Day
Freshwater Louse	Group 5	Still	Medium-large	Day
Freshwater Shrimp	Group 5	Still	Medium-large	Day
Corixa	Group 5	Still	Medium to small	Day
Leeches	Group 5	Still	Small to very large	Day

Artificial patterns
in alphabetical order

Adult Buzzer (Carnill)

Adult Midge (R. Walker)

Alder Fly

Alder Larva (Canham)

Amber Nymph (Bell)

August Dun (Woolley)

Beacon Beige (Dean)

Black Bear's Hair (Henry)

Black Gnat

Black Ground Beetle (Price)

Black Midge (Henderson)

Black and Peacock Spider

Black Silverhorn (Ronalds)

Blae and Black

Bloodworm (Wilshaw)

Bluebottle (Price)

Blue Upright (Austin)

Brown Sedge (T. Thomas)

B-WO (Jacques)

B-WO (Nice)

B-WO (C. F. Walker)

Caddis Larva (Boaze)

Caenis Spinner (Canham)

Caperer (Lunn)

Cased Caddis (Carnill)

Church Fry (Church)

Cinnamon Sedge

Claret Dun (Harris)

192

Claret Spinner

Collyer's Green or Brown Nymph

Coch-y-bonddu

Cockchafer (Henderson)

Corixa (Goddard)

Daddy-Long-Legs (R. Walker)

Damsel Fly (Canham)

Damsel Nymph (Henry)

Damsel Wiggle Nymph

Dark Spanish Needle (Pritt)

Dark Watchett (Pritt)

Deerstalker (Patterson)

Dogsbody (Powell)

Duck Fly (Harris)

Dusky Wood (Skues)

Emergent Midge (Price)

Eric's Beetle (Turner)

Ermine Moth

Floating Snail (Henry)

Footballer (Bucknall)

194

Freshwater Louse (Lapsley)

Funnel Dun (Patterson)

Gerroff (Goddard)

Ghost Swift Moth (R. Walker)

Goddard Caddis (G&H)

Goddard Smut

Green Lacewing (Price)

GRHE Winged

GRHE Nymph

Grafham Drone Fly

Grannom (P. Russell)

Greenwell's Glory

Green Peter

Grenadier (Dr Bell)

Grey Duster

Grey Wulff

Hackle Point Mayfly (Collyer)

Hatching Buzzer Pupa

Hatching Midge Pupa

Hatching Sedge Pupa

196

Hatching Sedge Pupa (Roberts)   Hawthorn Fly

Hoolet (Bucknall)   Houghton Ruby (Lunn)

HPB (Evans)   Iron Blue Dun (P. Russell)

Iron Blue Quill   Invicta

John Storey   July Dun (Skues)

Kite's Imperial

Lake Olive Dun

Large Red Spinner

Large Summer Dun (Price)

Large Summer Spinner

Last Hope Dark (Goddard)

Last Hope Light (Goddard)

Little Brown Sedge

Little Red Sedge (Skues)

Little Marryat

Longhorn Pupa (R. Walker)

Lunn's Particular

Lunn's Yellow Boy

Mallard and Claret

Mating Shrimp (Goddard)

Marabou Bloodworm (Price)

Marabou Midge Pupa (Price)

Marabou Leech (Price)

March Brown

March Brown Spider

Medium Stonefly (Price)

Mottled Sedge (J. Lane)

Muddler Minnow

Mylar Minnow (Brock)

Olive Quill

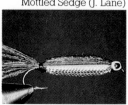

Ombudsman (Clarke)

Orange Quill

Otter Ruby Dun (Nice)

Pale Watery Dun

Pale Watery Spinner

Partridge and Orange

Peter Ross

Phantom Larva (Gathercole)

Phantom Pupa (Gathercole)

Pheasant Tail Nympn (Sawyer)

Pheasant Tail Spinner

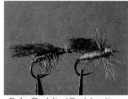
Poly Caddis (Goddard)

Poly May Dun (Goddard)

Poly May Spinner (Goddard)

Poly Rib C Pupa (Carnill)

Polystickle (R. Walker)

Pond Olive Dun (Price)

Pond Olive Spinner (Goddard)

Persuader (Goddard)

PVC Nymph (Goddard)

Red Mite (R. Walker)

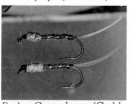
Red or Green Larva (Goddard)

Red Palmer

Red Spinner (Harris)

Red Spot Shrimp (Patterson)

Resting Midge (Price)

Rough Olive (Skues)

Sailor Beetle (Price)

Sand Caddis (R. Walker)

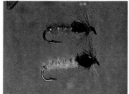
Sedge Pupa (Goddard)

Sepia Dun (Kite)

Sherry Spinner (Lunn)

Sharp's Favourite

Shorthorn Pupa (R. Walker)

Shredge (Knight)

Sinfoil's Fry

Silver Sedge (Halford)

Skating Midge (Price)

Snipe and Purple

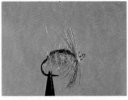
Soldier Beetle (Skues)

Stick Fly

Stonefly (Woolley)

Sunk Spinner (Patterson)

Super Grizzly (Goddard)

Suspender Hatching Midge

204

Suspender Hatching Nymph

Tadpolly (Goddard)

Terry's Terror

Tup's Indispensable

USD Dun (Clarke and Goddard)

USD Dun (Hairwing)

USD Hawthorn

USD Poly Spinner

Voss Bark's Nymph

Walker's Mayfly Dun

Walker's Sedge

Walker's Mayfly Nymph

Wickham's Fancy

Willow Fly (Ronalds)

Wooley Worm

Yellow May Dun (Price)

Yellow May Dun (Roberts)

Dressings for most of these flies will be found in:
A Dictionary of Trout Flies, by A. Courtney
Williams (A. & C. Black)
The New Illustrated Dictionary of Trout Flies, by
John Roberts (Unwin Hyman)
Robson's Guide, by Kenneth Robson (Beekay
Publishers)

Bibliography

The British Caddis Flies, by Martin E. Mosely
Caddis Larvae, by Norman E. Hickin
Freshwater Life of the British Isles, by John Clegg
A Dictionary of Trout Flies, by A. Courtney
Williams
New Illustrated Dictionary of Trout Flies, by John
Roberts
Robson's Guide of Stillwater Trout Flies, by
Kenneth Robson
Rough Stream Trout Flies, by S. D. (Taff) Price
Taff Price's Stillwater Flies (Books 1 to 3), by S. D.
(Taff) Price
Trout Fly Recognition, by John Goddard
Trout Flies of Stillwater, by John Goddard

Freshwater Biological Association booklets
A Revised Key to the British Water Bugs, by T. T.
Macan
*A Key to the Adults and Nymphs of British
Stoneflies*, by H. B. N. Hynes
A Key to Crustacea: Malacostraca, by Hynes,
Macan and Williams
*A Key to the simulidae in the larval, pupal and
adult stages* by Lewis Davies
A Key to the Adults of the British Trichoptera, by
T. T. Macan
A Key to British Dixidae, by R. H. L. Disney
A Key to the Nymphs of British Ephemeroptera, by
T. T. Macan
A Key to Adults of the British Ephemeroptera, by
J. M. Elliott and U. H. Humpesch
*A Key to Adult Males of British Chironomidae (Part
1)*, by L. C. V. Pinder
*A Key to Adult Males of British Chironomidae (Part
2)*, by L. C. V. Pinder

Handbooks for the Identification of British Insects
published by the Royal Entomological Society of
London
Vol. IX (Part 2), Diptera, by R. L. Coe, Paul
Freeman and P. F. Mattingly

Index

Page numbers in bold type indicate either an artificial fly or a reference to a pattern imitative of a natural fly.